Maldives

Roseline NgCheong-Lum

Marshall Cavendish
Benchmark
New York

PICTURE CREDITS
Cover: © James L. Stanfield / Getty Images
Ace Stock Limited/Alamy: 124 • Amal Jayasinghe/AFP/Getty Images: 14 • Asif Hassan/AFP/Getty Images: 106
• Associated Press Photo: 26 • Audrius Tomonis: 135 • B. Gain, G. Frysinger/Travel-Images.com: 115, 116 •
Emmanuel Dunand/AFP/Getty Images: 71, 89 • EyesWideOpen/Getty Images: 47, 107 • Felix Hug/Lonely Planet
Images: 1, 7, 63, 66, 86, 118 • Focus Team, Italy: 92, 96, 103 • Hassan N/Alamy: 115, 119 • Hassan Najmy/
Alamy: 116 • HBL Network: 12 • Hilarie Kavanagh/Getty Images: 76 • James Lyon/Lonely Planet Images:
62, 69, 72, 80, 123, 129 • John Borthwick/Lonely Planet Images: 58, 75 • Jon Nicholson/Getty Images: 48 •
Lakruwan Wanniarachchi/AFP/Getty Images: 27, 28, 34, 35, 36, 70, 113, 120, 127 • Michele Westmorland/ The
Image bank/ Getty Images: 119 • Northwind Picture Archives: 19, 22 • Pankaj Nangia/Bloomberg/Getty Images:
25 • photolibrary: 3, 5, 6, 8, 9, 10, 11, 15, 16, 24, 31, 38, 41, 43, 45, 46, 51, 52, 61, 64, 65, 68, 73, 74, 78, 81, 82,
84, 85, 90, 91, 93, 94, 95, 97, 98, 99, 101, 102, 104, 108, 114, 121, 130, 131 • prpix.com.au/Getty Images: 110 •
Sakis Papadopoulos/Getty Images: 50 • Sena Vidanagama/AFP/Getty Images: 33, 44, 53, 77 • Staeven Vallak/
Lonely Planet Images: 56, 79 • Topham Picturepoint: 83, 125 • travelib/Alamy: 112 • travelib prime/Alamy: 18
• Trip Photographic Library: 13, 40, 87, 122, 128 • Will Salter/Lonely Planet Images: 57, 105, 126

PRECEDING PAGE
A Maldivian girl from the North Male Atoll.

Publisher (U.S.): Michelle Bisson
Editors: Deborah Grahame-Smith, Stephanie Pee
Copyreader: Tara Tomczyk
Designers: Nancy Sabato, Benson Tan
Cover picture researcher: Connie Gardner
Picture researchers: Thomas Khoo, Joshua Ang

Marshall Cavendish Benchmark
99 White Plains Road
Tarrytown, NY 10591
Website: www.marshallcavendish.us

© Times Media Private Limited 1999
© Marshall Cavendish International (Asia) Private Limited 2011
® "Cultures of the World" is a registered trademark of Times Publishing Limited.

Originated and designed by Times Media Private Limited
An imprint of Marshall Cavendish International (Asia) Private Limited
A member of Times Publishing Limited

Marshall Cavendish is a trademark of Times Publishing Limited.

All Internet sites were correct and accurate at the time of printing. All monetary figures in this publication
are in U.S. dollars.

Library of Congress Cataloging-in-Publication Data
NgCheong-Lum, Roseline, 1962-
  Maldives / Roseline Ng Cheong-Lum. — [2nd ed.].
      p. cm. — (Cultures of the world)
  Includes bibliographical references and index.
  Summary: "Provides comprehensive information on the geography, history,
wildlife, governmental structure, economy, cultural diversity, peoples,
religion, and culture of Maldives"—Provided by publisher.
  ISBN 978-1-60870-217-6
  1. Maldives—Juvenile literature. I. Title.
  DS349.9.M34N45 2011
  954.95 dc22   2010019746

Printed in China
7 6 5 4 3 2 1

CONTENTS

INTRODUCTION

RISING OUT OF THE INDIAN OCEAN LIKE A PRECIOUS NECKLACE, Maldives has always fascinated travelers. Called the "flower of the Indies" by Marco Polo and "one of the wonders of the world" by the 14th-century traveler Mohammed Ibn Battuta, the archipelago used to draw traders shuttling between East and West. The traders stopped for fresh supplies and cowry shells, which were the major form of currency then. Today Maldives attracts travelers in search of peace and tranquility.

For the islanders, however, life is hardly a holiday. Their life is a harsh one: hours spent at sea fishing or in gardens coaxing the soil to grow some vegetables. But, with their steadfast Muslim faith, they face every day with renewed hope and energy.

With global warming causing sea levels to rise, many of the Maldives islands could become submerged within this century. Maldives is doing its best to educate the rest of the world on the perils of pollution since its destiny depends on finding a solution.

GEOGRAPHY

Crystal clear waters and sapphire skies attract many tourists to the Maldives every year.

MALDIVES IS A CHAIN OF SMALL coral islands in the Indian Ocean. The country's name comes from the ancient Sanskrit language and means "garland of islands."

Scattered over an area of 34,750 square miles (90,003 square kilometers) in the Indian Ocean, the 1,190 small tropical islands only add up to 115 square miles (298 square km). Maldives is unique in that the sea forms 99.669 percent of its territory.

Maldives appears in the *Guinness Book of Records* as the flattest country in the world. No island is higher than 7 feet (2 m) above

The Maldives is the smallest Asian country in both population and area. With an average ground level of 4 feet, 11 inches (1.5 meters), it is the lowest country on the planet. It is also the country with the lowest highest point in the world.

An airplane making its descent onto one of Maldives's northern islands.

sea level. The islands have no hills or rivers. Only about 200 islands are inhabited.

The Maldivian archipelago lies about 217 miles (350 km), the shortest distance from the mainland, south of India. But the people have more affinity with Sri Lanka, which is 460 miles (740 km) to the east. Until recently the only way to get to Maldives has been via Sri Lanka.

THE MALDIVIAN ARCHIPELAGO

The archipelago consists of 26 atolls, each one formed by a coral reef. For administrative purposes, however, the government recognizes only 20 of them. In the middle of each atoll is a lagoon. Islands rise from the outer reef and are protected by their own reef. Deep channels in the reef allow boats to move from one atoll to the other. Each atoll consists of about 5 to 10 inhabited islands and 20 to 60 uninhabited ones. All 20 official atolls have both an administrative as well as a traditional name. In addition the government uses the letters of the Maldivian alphabet to refer to them.

The first tourist resorts were developed in North Male Atoll, and most of the country's 70 resorts are found here.

An aerial view of the South Male atoll. The bulk of Maldives's territory is made up of water.

The capital city of Male.

MALE

The most important atoll in Maldives is Male (MA-lay) Atoll. Consisting of North and South Male atolls, it lies halfway down the archipelago. The atoll has 105 uninhabited and 12 inhabited islands. Male, the capital, is on the southern tip of North Male Atoll. Next to it is Hulhule, the country's international airport, which was created by flattening an entire island. Male Atoll is the political and commercial hub of the country. Male and the other central atolls support most of the Maldivian population.

THE NORTHERN ATOLLS

The northern atolls are located near India, and Indian influence is stronger there. Islands in the northern atolls are closer together, and communication between them is easy. They are the least touched by tourism and seem rather remote from the center of activity in Male. Northern atolls are characterized

A beach on the Baa Atoll, one of the most isolated atolls in the Maldives.

by mangroves and are frequently struck by heavy storms. They were the most affected during the 2004 Indian Ocean tsunami. The northernmost inhabited island of Maldives is Thuraakunu in Haa Alif Atoll. As for Faridhoo in Haa Dhaal Atoll, it holds the distinction of being the highest natural point in the Maldives, at about 9 feet (3 m) above the sea level. The island of Utheemu has a special place in the Maldivian's heart because it was the birthplace of national hero Mohamed Thakurufaanu, and it is now an important pilgrimage center for Maldivians from all over the archipelago. Fulhadhoo, Fehendhoo, and Goidhoo in Baa Atoll are so isolated that they have been used as open prisons for exiles since 1962.

THE SOUTHERN ATOLLS

The southern atolls are separated from the central atolls by the One-and-a-Half-Degree Channel, the broadest and the most dangerous stretch of water in Maldives. The channel gets its name from its location, one and a half degrees north of the equator. The southern atolls are isolated from Male, and

A beach resort on one of the southern atolls.

an unsuccessful secession movement was active in the 1960s. The southern atolls are closer to Sri Lanka, and the inhabitants are different from the rest of the Maldivian population. One of the best-known southern islands is Gan, which served as a British military base from World War II until 1976. Gan is also the largest island in the archipelago. The Maldivian government views the southern atolls as being ripe for tourism development and has ambitious plans for the region. In the next decade each atoll will host at least one tourist resort.

ATOLL FORMATION

The Maldives islands lie on an underwater volcanic mountain ridge. The atolls are formed when coral growth produces a fringing reef around each volcanic landmass. As the reef grows taller, the land subsides until the volcano disappears completely. Only the reef is left, encircling a lagoon of water where the volcano used to be. This reef continues to grow, and the higher parts eventually become islands.

One of the largest atolls in the world is Huvadhoo, which lies just above the equator. Its lagoon covers an area of 864,868 square miles (2,240 square km).

An atoll is usually oval in shape, with most of the islands located on the outer edges of the reef, where coral growth is more vigorous. Some atolls also have islands inside the lagoon, but these tend to be smaller. Reeftop atolls have no interior lagoon but are composed of a single island covering most of the reef platform.

The composition of each atoll can be altered by ocean currents, storms, or monsoonal changes. Erosion causes many islands to change their shape and size. In some drastic cases, the whole island vanishes into the ocean. On the other hand, whole islands can appear from nowhere after a storm. The islands of Aahura and Udhafushi were formed during storms that hit Maldives in 1955 and 1987, respectively.

CLIMATE

Because Maldives is in the tropics, there is little variation in temperature throughout the year. The weather is hot and humid most of the time, with daytime highs of 86°F (30°C) dropping to 75°F (24°C) at night. Sea breezes keep the air moving and help temper the humidity.

A pretty rainbow appears after a storm.

The year is divided into two monsoon periods. The northeast monsoon lasts from November to March; these are the drier months of the year. The southwest monsoon from June to August brings strong winds and storms. In May 1991, tidal waves resulting from violent monsoon winds swept away thousands of houses and flooded large areas. The damage was estimated at $30 million.

The average annual rainfall is 84 inches (213 centimeters), with the south receiving more rain than the north.

AN ISLAND CAPITAL

The capital of Maldives, Male, is an entire island. Male has been the cultural, political, and business center of Maldives throughout its history. The island is small, only 1.2 miles (2 km) long and 0.62 miles (1 km) wide. With a permanent population of 104,000 and thousands of daily visitors, it is the second most populated island in the world. Land reclamation has increased the size of the island considerably, but it still faces great population pressure.

The Male International Airport on Hulhule Island.

Male is divided into four districts: Henveiru, Maafanu, Machangolhi, and Galolhu. Henveiru in the northeast overlooks the harbor. It is a rather wealthy neighborhood, with government offices and elaborate villas lining Marine Drive, the main street of the island. Maafanu covers the northwestern end of the island. It houses the Presidential Palace, some foreign embassies, and most of Male's hotels. Situated in the south of the island, Machangolhi has Male's main shopping area. Galolhu, in central Male, is where most residents live.

Male's skyline is dominated by the three-story Islamic Center. Opened in 1984 this huge golden-domed complex houses the Grand Friday Mosque, an Islamic library, a conference hall, and a number of classrooms. Many other mosques are dotted around Male, with the most significant being the Friday Mosque. Built in 1656 it contains intricate carvings and the tombs of ancient Maldivian heroes.

The artificial island of Hulhumale was built to ease traffic congestion in the capital city of Male, and also to fight against rising sea levels.

As the country develops rapidly, Male is constantly changing. Many buildings are torn down to make way for taller ones. Land reclamation goes on in the south and west, and the breakwaters prevent the northern area from being washed away in a storm.

To relieve population pressure on Male, the building of a manmade island started in 1997 on a reef 0.8 mile (1.3 km) off the northeast coast of Male. By pouring sand and coral on top of the reef, a completely manmade island of the same area as the capital was created. Hulhumale was inaugurated in 2004, and the northern section is now a fully functioning town. In the long term expansion works will engulf the island of Farukolhufushi to the north and double the area of Hulhumale.

FLORA AND FAUNA

Maldivian soil is quite poor and does not support much vegetation. Altogether there are 583 plant species, of which half are cultivated. One interesting

Coconut palms lining the beach on one of the Maldivian islands. The coconut palm is the national tree of Maldives.

feature of Maldivian flora is that almost all the common native species are identical to those of Pacific coral islands. The most common tree is the coconut palm, the national tree of Maldives. Breadfruit, almond, screw pine, casuarina, and banyan trees can be found on the larger islands. Many tropical flowers grow in profusion. Bougainvillea, frangipani, and hibiscus turn the gardens and parks into colorful and scented havens. The national flower of Maldives is the pink rose, which is not native to the tropics.

Wildlife is also limited in Maldives. Small animals and insects make up the land fauna. The most conspicuous animal is the flying fox, a large type of bat. Cats, chickens, and goats are the only domestic animals. There are no dogs in Maldives because the Islamic faith prohibits any contact with the animal. Insects and reptiles include butterflies, scorpions, wasps, lizards, and turtles.

The flying fox is actually a large bat that feeds on fruit.

The coconut palm is truly the tree of life in Maldives. The islanders have found a use for every part of the tree, from the fruit to the trunk and leaves. The coconut provides food with its milk and flesh. The milk of the kurumba *(KOO-room-bah) or young coconut makes a refreshing drink. It is also used in cooking. The sweet and tender flesh goes into curries and cakes. The husk is turned into coir and rope. The sap is tapped from the stalk at the crown of the palm and made into a drink. When boiled it becomes a type of syrup. Coconut oil is extracted from the ripe coconuts.*

Coconut fronds are woven to make roofs, mats, and walls. The trunks are made into boats and are used to make houses and furniture. Anything left over is burned as fuel.

MARINE LIFE

The waters around Maldives teem with marine life. More than 200 types of coral live on the reefs surrounding the atolls. In the sandy lagoons the corals are small and delicate. On the reef edge, where sunlight is less intense and currents are stronger, they are large and robust. Coral colonies come in all shapes and sizes, forming fans, leaves, columns, arches, and caves. Most of them are very colorful.

The most common fish in Maldivian waters is the parrotfish. Brightly colored, it has a beak and swims as if it is flapping wings. Other fascinating fish include clown fish, butterfly fish, angelfish, and triggerfish. In the lower depths live sharks, tuna, barracuda, rays, and eels. The whale shark is the largest fish in the world. Dolphins, especially the dark gray bottlenose dolphin, are also abundant. Among the endangered marine species is the giant leatherback turtle. Four species of turtle nest in Maldives: green, olive ridley, hawksbill, and loggerhead. The hawksbill used to be plentiful in Maldives, but numbers have declined due to hunting.

More than 5,000 species of shells are found on the reefs. Maldives is best known for cowry shells. For many centuries the humble cowry was the most valuable product of Maldives. It was used as currency by countries bordering the Indian Ocean.

THOSE COMMEMORATED HERE
DIED IN THE SERVICE
OF THEIR COUNTRY
THE MORTAL REMAINS OF SOME
WERE COMMITTED TO FIRE

HISTORY

जिन्होंने अपने देश की सेवा में
प्राण त्यागे उन की स्मृति में।
कुछ व्यक्तियों के नश्वर अवशेषों का
दाह संस्कार किया गया और अन्य
जत्थ अटोल में ही दफनाए गए

A war memorial for those who died defending
the territory

MALDIVES'S EARLY HISTORY IS shrouded in mystery. According to one legend Sinhalese women were the first inhabitants of the islands called Mahiladipa, or "the islands of women."

In 2008,
Maldivians were
able to take
part in free and
fair multiparty
elections.

The friendly women welcomed travelers and bore their children. It is probable that the first settlers arrived from Sri Lanka and India before 500 B.C. However, the islands were well known to seafarers as early as 2000 B.C. Maldives was an important stop on trading routes between East and West, and Egyptians, Phoenicians, Romans, Arabs, and Indians all called at the islands at one time or another. Here they exchanged food and spices for cowry shells, the money used by the ancient people of the Middle East and India.

According to ethnologist and author Thor Heyerdahl, a mythical people called the Redin were the first to settle in Maldives. Not much is known about them except that they were light-skinned giants who worshiped the sun. In 500 B.C. they were either chased away or became assimilated with the Indians and Sinhalese who came to the islands. Maldives was then ruled by a series of Buddhist kings and queens whose history is now mixed with legend.

Right: A representation of a sun-worshiping king on his throne.

CONVERSION TO ISLAM

Recorded history in Maldives begins with the arrival of Islam in 1153 B.C. According to Mohammed Ibn Battuta, a Moroccan traveler who visited the islands in the 14th century, a sea monster used to terrorize the people, demanding the sacrifice of a virgin girl once a month. In 1153 a Muslim visitor named Abul Barakath Yusuf Al Barbary decided to take the place of the chosen girl. He chanted Koranic verses all night and the monster was never seen again. After witnessing this miracle, the Maldivian ruler immediately converted to Islam, taking the name of Sultan Mohammed Ibn Abdullah. He decreed Islam to be the sole religion of the whole country. It took almost 60 years before all the islands converted to the new religion. Sultan Mohammed Ibn Abdullah founded the Malei Dynasty, which would rule the country for 169 years, but he himself disappeared in 1166 on a pilgrimage to Mecca.

Quaint as the story of the conversion may be, it was certainly for political motives that the Buddhist king of Maldives became Muslim. In the 12th century Buddhist Sri Lanka was growing more and more powerful, and Sultan Mohammed must have been afraid of being annexed by his much larger neighbor. Converting to Islam earned him the support of the Muslim states bordering the Indian Ocean, thus keeping Sri Lanka at bay.

THE SULTANATE

Six dynasties ruled Maldives from 1153 to 1968, although not continuously. The Malei Dynasty produced 16 monarchs from 1153 to 1321. Two sultans and three sultanas of the Veeru Umaru Dynasty then reigned for the next 75 years. The third great dynasty was that of the Hilali. Twenty-four sultans ruled over 170 years before Maldives fell to outside forces.

The post of sultan was never hereditary; a council elected the sultan. Women were also chosen to rule as sultanas, and there were always women on the ruling councils. Sultana Khadeeja Rehendhi Kanbaidhi Kilege, a remarkable woman, held power on three different occasions. She first became sultana in 1342 after the death of her younger brother, the previous sultan.

THOR HEYERDAHL AND THE MALDIVIAN MYSTERY

Thor Heyerdahl, a well-known Norwegian explorer, became fascinated with Maldives after seeing pictures of a stone statue that was uncannily similar to the figures he had previously investigated on Easter Island in the Pacific Ocean. In the mid-1980s the Maldivian government allowed him to conduct archaeological research on some ancient sites, and he unearthed many artifacts that shed light on the early settlement of the islands. His discoveries lend credence to the theory that Maldives was inhabited by a well-developed Hindu and Buddhist society whose history was never documented or whose records were completely destroyed when the country adopted Islam.

One of the most important archaeological finds was the buried temple complex on the island of Nilandhoo in the central atoll of Faaf. Evidence suggests that there were seven temples altogether and that they were certainly Hindu because of the Hindu phallic sculptures recovered around the site. The complex is of impressive dimensions, and the temples were built of beautifully cut stones placed over a foundation of coral sand. They were shaped like pyramids. Heyerdahl also came across many limestone sculptures of Hindu gods and demons on several other islands.

On the uninhabited island of Gan in Gaaf Dhaal Atoll, Heyerdahl found evidence of Maldives's Buddhist past. In the middle of the jungle stands an impressive 3,000-year-old pyramid of enormous proportions. The explorer believes that it was a stepped pyramid with ceremonial ramps on four sides, much like the ancient pyramids of Mesopotamia and pre-Columbian America. Among the artifacts recovered were the foot of a sitting Buddha, a stone bull, and two lions. The nearby island of Fua Mulaku also contains several hawitta *(HA-wit-tah). Called Redin's Hill by the islanders, these mounds of stone are the remnants of Buddhist bell-shaped temples. Another important site is the sunken bath made from stones of different sizes. They fit so well that it is impossible to slide a knife blade between them.*

Despite all his discoveries, Heyerdahl was not able to solve the mystery of the Redin people, and hence the title of the book he wrote about his investigations was named The Maldive Mystery. *He suggested that they were sun worshipers, similar to the people of ancient Peru and Mexico. He based this theory on the fact that many mosques built on the remains of ancient temples faced the sun instead of Mecca, the holy Islamic land where the Prophet Muhammad was born.*

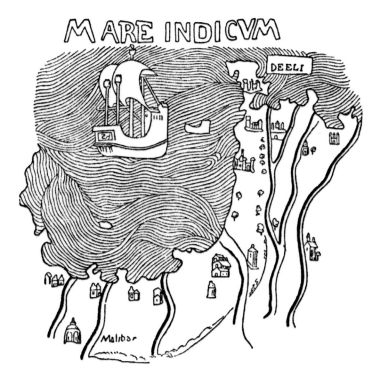

MARE INDICVM

DEELI

Malabar

The route from the coast of Malabar to Maldives, as depicted on explorer Fra' Mauro's map.

Many scholars believe that she murdered him. In 1363 she was overthrown by her husband. But she managed to kill him and took back the throne. In 1373 her position was usurped by her second husband. The latter was also killed, and Khadeeja returned to power until her death in 1380.

THE PORTUGUESE OCCUPATION

At the beginning of the 16th century the Portuguese, who had already established a base in India, started to look at Maldives for its strategic location on the trade routes and its abundant supply of cowry shells. Three attempts to invade the islands were unsuccessful, but in 1558 a powerful Portuguese army under the command of Captain Andrea Andreas killed Sultan Ali VI. They were helped by the former sultan, Hassan IX, who had fled to India and converted to Christianity after a disagreement with the council of ministers. Andrea Andreas installed himself as the ruler of Maldives on behalf of Dom Emanuel, the Christian name of Hassan IX.

The Maldivians did not submit meekly to the occupation. Mohammed Thakurufaanu from the northern island of Utheemu organized a band of guerrilla warriors to conduct raids against the Portuguese defenses in Male. After several years he realized that he could not oust the Portuguese on his own and sought help from the Rajah of Malabar in India. In 1573 Thakurufaanu, together with the Indian forces, launched an attack on Male and, with the help of the islanders, liberated the country from the cruel occupiers. For the next 12 years Thakurufaanu reigned as sultan and founded the Utheemu Dynasty that lasted 127 years. The day of the liberation is now celebrated as National Day each year, and Thakurufaanu is venerated as the greatest national hero of Maldivian history.

BRITISH PROTECTORATE

Their success in helping the Maldivians fight the Portuguese gave ideas to the Malabars, who tried to invade the islands several times in the next two centuries. They finally succeeded in 1752, with the help of some Maldivians. Malabar rule, however, lasted only four months before the wily Hassan Manikufaan drove them out. This was the only other time in Maldivian history that the islands were ruled by outsiders. Manikufaan became sultan in 1759, founding the Huraage Dynasty that ruled the country until it became a republic.

Toward the end of the 18th century the British became very active in the Indian Ocean and took over Sri Lanka in 1796. Because Maldives had good historical ties with Sri Lanka, relations with the British were smooth. In 1887 Sultan Mohammed Mueenuddin II signed an agreement with Queen Victoria to turn Maldives into a British protectorate in return for an annual tribute. Two main reasons prompted this move: Some Indian merchants had acquired a monopoly on foreign trade, and the sultan was afraid they would gain control over all the islands; and putting Maldives under the protection of the British Crown meant that the British would not colonize the islands.

The protectorate worked very well for the Maldivian rulers who were left to govern the country as autocrats. The British had no power to interfere in internal matters and could only control foreign relations. What they were more interested in, especially after Sri Lanka and India became independent in 1948, was the development of a military base on the southern island of Gan.

THE REPUBLIC

In 1932 a constitution was adopted for the first time in Maldivian history that curtailed the powers of the sultan. When the elderly sultan Abdul

The 15 years of Portuguese occupation were the darkest in Maldivian history. Men were treated as slaves, women were violated, and a reign of terror extended to the outer atolls. The captain of the Portuguese forces, Andrea Andreas, also decreed that all Maldivians had to convert to Christianity or be put to death.

A painting of Queen Victoria. She ruled the British Empire from 1837 to 1901.

Majeed Didi came to power in 1943, he left the government of the country in the hands of his prime minister, Mohammed Amin Didi. The latter set about nationalizing the fish export industry and modernizing the country. Maldives was declared a republic in 1953, and Amin Didi became the country's first president. Regarded as the father of modern Maldives, he reformed the education system, revived interest in the Maldivian language and literature, and gave women a larger role in society. But his policies were too drastic, and he was overthrown a year later. Amin Didi died in 1954 after being beaten by a mob during a riot over food shortages.

INDEPENDENCE

The sultanate was restored after Amin Didi's death and lasted until 1968. The British started developing their air base on Gan in 1956, bringing work and much prosperity to the southern atolls. When Ibrahim Nasir became prime minister in 1957, he called for a review of the agreement to lease Gan to the British. This angered the inhabitants of Addu and Huvadhoo atolls. In 1959, claiming that they were ill-treated by the central government, the two atolls, together with Gnaviyani, declared independence as the United Suvadive Islands. Three years later Nasir sent gunboats to the southern atolls, and the elected president of the Suvadive Islands was forced to flee to the Seychelles.

On July 26, 1965, the British lifted the protectorate, and Maldives became an independent sovereign nation. British forces, however, remained on Gan until 1976. Following a referendum in 1968, the sultanate was definitively abolished, and a new republic was established. Nasir was elected president,

Born in Male in 1937, Maumoon Abdul Gayoom's intelligence was apparent when he received a scholarship at the age of 10, becoming the youngest person to be sent overseas by the government. He went on to study in Sri Lanka and Egypt, where he obtained a master's degree in Islamic studies. He also studied law and philosophy.

Before being elected president in 1978, Gayoom worked in various government departments and was Maldives's first permanent representative to the United Nations. He was a lecturer in Islamic law and philosophy in Nigeria from 1969 to 1971. In a policy statement in 1979 he committed himself to give greater freedom to the people and to follow democratic procedures. Gayoom was himself a victim of repression during the Nasir years when he was banished from Male in 1973. During his 30 years in power, he brought political and economic stability to the islands through constitutional changes and sound economic policies. While turning the Maldives into a tourism powerhouse and bringing much-needed foreign exchange into the country, he also led a repressive Muslim system that did not tolerate dissent. Despite promising greater freedoms to the population, he ruled as an autocrat, exiling anyone who did not agree with his policies and installing family and friends in the top rungs of authority.

One of the achievements of Maumoon Abdul Gayoom in the international arena was to highlight the plight of small island states in the face of increased industrialization. He was one of the first world leaders to caution against global warming. Taking part in forums and international conferences, he tirelessly repeated his message that the industrialized world is accountable to small island states for the rise in sea levels, and that countries such as Maldives are in danger of disappearing. As he states in his biography, he is "a man for all islands."

and he ruled for 10 years, serving two terms. By 1978 dissatisfaction over the spiraling prices of food led the population to protest against the president. Fearing for his life, Nasir resigned and fled to Singapore.

Maumoon Abdul Gayoom was elected president to replace Nasir. Adopting a more consultative and open style of government, he was immensely popular and survived three coup attempts—in 1980, 1983, and 1988. Under his leadership, Maldives opened up to tourism and experienced good economic growth. In the 1990s Maldives developed at a fast pace, with the country being linked by a modern telecommunications system, electricity reaching 90 percent of all households, and Maldivians in the outer atolls gaining access to secondary education and health care. Because people enjoyed prosperity under his rule, Gayoom was reelected six times.

DEMOCRACY AT LAST

The early 21st century saw dissatisfaction spreading among the Maldivian population. The long-promised political freedoms had not materialized,

The aftermath of rioting in the city of Male in 2003.

and the wealth generated by tourism was slow to trickle down to the people of the atolls. Moreover both the Male population and those living in the atolls had to put up with a degraded environment and the problems associated with fast-paced development.

A Maldivian woman casting her vote during the 2008 elections.

In 2003 rioting erupted in Male, with the stoning of the Parliament building as well as the burning of several police stations. In response Gayoom proposed several political reforms, including multi-party presidential elections, a two-term limit for the president, and allowing political parties. August 2004 witnessed more violence when the authorities cracked down harshly on a pro-democracy meeting. That same year the Indian Ocean tsunami caused havoc throughout the archipelago, submerging several islands and killing more than 100 persons. Many tourist resorts were destroyed, leading to a drastic drop in tourism earnings. More than 11,000 people lost their homes, and many have not been resettled.

Finally, in 2005, the first glimmer of democracy appeared when political parties were legalized. In a 2007 referendum, the Maldivian population voted for a presidential system of government similar to that of the United States. In August 2008 Maldives received a new constitution, and the first-ever multiparty elections took place in October 2008. In a runoff election between incumbent Gayoom and Mohammed Nasheed, a former political prisoner, the latter took 54 percent of the votes and was installed into office in November 2008. Promising sweeping reforms and vowing to crack down on corruption, the first freely elected president of the Maldives quickly set about liberalizing the administration, privatizing state-owned enterprises, and pledging to make the Maldives a carbon-neutral country. Many challenges remain, though, such as strengthening democracy and combating poverty and drug abuse.

GOVERNMENT

Supporters of the Maldivian party cheering during an election rally.

MALDIVES IS A democratic republic that is inspired by Islam. The present constitution, adopted in 1968, has been amended several times, in 1970, 1972, 1975, and most recently in 2008. It provides for the basic rights of the people, such as freedom of speech and assembly, equality before the law, and the right to own property.

Nevertheless the various governments have not always upheld these rights, in particular freedom of speech and assembly. The latest constitution provides for a separation of powers among the legislative, executive, and judicial branches, and includes a Bill of Rights for the Maldivian citizen. It also gives women the right to become the president of the country.

The people of Maldives are called Maldivian citizens. Anyone over the age of 18 has the right to vote in presidential as well as in legislative elections and to run for office. The 2008 constitution stipulates that only Muslims can be Maldivian citizens. When it came into effect, 3,000 persons suddenly lost their citizenship.

THE LEGISLATIVE STRUCTURE

The government of Maldives is composed of a unicameral assembly called the People's Majlis (MADGE-liss). Made up of 77 representatives,

Maldives's first constitution provided for a democratic government with executive, legislative, and judicial branches. In practice, however, the president held sway over every aspect of the country. The latest constitution of 2008 spells out clearly the separation of powers between the various branches of government.

the Majlis enacts laws and approves the annual budget. The Maldivian electorate is made up of 77 single-member constituencies, and each eligible citizen votes for one person only. The Maldivian constitution divides the archipelago geographically into administrative zones, and these are further divided into constituencies, depending on the size of the population. Each member of the Majlis represents a maximum of 5,000 people. However, due to discrepancy in settlements, some constituencies may have several times the number of voters as others. Candidates for election to the People's Majlis can stand as representatives of political parties or as independents.

The Special Majlis is a separate body that gathers on a temporary basis to make amendments to the constitution. It is made up of cabinet ministers, the 77 members of the People's Majlis, and a number of elected members as well as presidential appointees.

The head of state is the president, who is elected by direct and universal suffrage. Candidates have to be Maldivian citizens born of Maldivian parents, Sunni Muslim, and at least 35 years old. Presidential elections are held every five years and do not coincide with legislative elections. The constitution places a limit of two terms on the presidential office. The president appoints the cabinet of ministers in charge of governing the country as well as the High Court judges, and the constitution also makes the president the guardian of Islam in the country. Like in many other countries, the Maldivian president is also in charge of national defense. At present the cabinet is composed of 14 ministers. These ministers need not be elected members of the Majlis. The president simply selects the best people for the job.

THE JUDICIARY

The legal system in Maldives is based on the Islamic Sharia law combined with some English common law, in particular in the area of commercial law. The head of the judiciary is the chief justice, who is usually a highly respected Islamic scholar. The chief justice, together with two other judges, presides over the Supreme Court, which also serves as the court of appeal. All three are appointed by the president after consultation with the Judicial Service

NATIONAL SYMBOLS

The Maldivian flag consists of a green rectangle surrounded by a red border. In the center is a white crescent with the tips facing away from the flag post. The red border symbolizes the blood of the Maldivians who fought for the freedom of their country. The green rectangle represents life, progress, and prosperity. The white crescent in the center of the flag denotes the Islamic faith of the nation.

The national emblem consists of a coconut palm rising from a crescent and a star, and flanked by two national flags. Underneath is a scroll with the traditional title of the country written in Arabic. The coconut palm represents the livelihood of the country because of its many uses in daily life. The crescent and star represent Islam, while the two flags are symbols of authority. The words Ad-Dawlat Al-Mahaldheebiyya written on the scroll mean "The State of Maldives" in Arabic. The emblem is usually reproduced on a light blue background to represent the importance of the ocean to Maldives.

Commission. The attorney general advises the president and the cabinet on matters of law. Every inhabited island has its own court of law. Male has eight courts.

ATOLL ADMINISTRATION

The archipelago is divided into 20 administrative units, composed of the island of Male and 19 atolls. Although they are called atolls, they do not coincide with the geographical atolls. Some administrative atolls are actually made up of more than one atoll, while others are only half an atoll. The 19 atolls are Alif, Baa, Dhaal, Faaf, Gaaf Alif, Gaaf Dhaal, Gnaviyani, Haa Alif, Haa Dhaal, Kaafu, Laamu, Lhaviyani, Meemu, Noonu, Raa, Seenu, Shaviyani, Thaa, and Vaavu.

Each atoll is governed by an atoll chief called *atolhu varin* (AH-toh-loo VAH-rin). This person functions as the governor of a province. He receives legal advice from the *ghaazee* (HAR-zee), the religious head of the atoll. The atoll chief is appointed by the president and tends to come from an influential family residing in the capital of the atoll. He is responsible for the economic and political direction of the atoll.

Every inhabited island is supervised by a *katheeb* (KAH-teeb), who is an official appointed by the government. The island chief, usually a distinguished island citizen, has a number of full-time officials, called *kuda katheeb* (KOO-da KAH-teeb), to help him run the island. They in turn work together with an island council. The island chief is an important personage; any islander summoned by the *katheeb's* office would go immediately. Justice is delivered by the local magistrate, but serious cases are referred to the courts in Male.

As part of the decentralization and regionalization process, the new Maldivian government has grouped the 20 administrative atolls into seven provinces, each headed by a state minister. The ultimate goal is to achieve a three-tier local government, with the sector ministries at the national level, province and atoll offices at the regional level, and the island office at the island level. This will ensure that local policies are coordinated with national policies, thus streamlining the economy and reducing the social, economic, and development disparities between Male and the rest of the country.

NATIONAL DEFENSE

The Maldives National Defense Force (MNDF) is responsible for the defense of the country. Made up of the Coast Guard and Infantry Units, its mission is to preserve internal security and patrol the country's territorial waters for smugglers and illegal fishermen. The more important component, the Coast Guard, also responds to maritime distress calls and takes part in search and rescue operations at sea. The Infantry Units take charge of combat situations and can operate both on land and at sea. The nonmilitary component of the MNDF, the Fire and Rescue Service, provides firefighting and rescue services to the population.

Maldivian soldiers loading bottled water onto a ferry bound for fellow Maldivians living on an isolated atoll after the 2004 tsunami.

The Maldives Police Service is responsible for law and order in the islands. There are 19 police stations throughout the archipelago, and police officers are deployed to patrol the villages and respond to crime situations. The police also guard the airports as well as offer protection for the president and other important officials.

There is no military draft in Maldives, but all Maldivians 18 and older may join the MNDF on a voluntary basis.

CRIME AND PUNISHMENT

Maldives follows a moderate version of the Muslim Sharia law that does not use extreme physical punishment. Although the crime rate is low, many actions are classified as being criminal in nature. Most of the crimes investigated in Maldives concern inappropriate sexual relations and the consumption of alcohol. Petty theft and white-collar crimes are on the rise, as is drug consumption. Male residents are most concerned about the security of their homes as urban development leads to more cases of housebreaking and burglary. Gang violence is another cause for concern for the urban police force, with many people fearing for their personal safety in the streets of Male at night.

Maldivian police patroling the waterfront in Male.

According to the Human Rights Commission of the Maldives, the rising crime rate is due to the inability of the authorities to enforce sentences and to the lengthy trial process. Most criminals are repeat offenders who have not been jailed even after sentencing, and failure to enforce sentences on juveniles has led to young offenders falling deeper into a life of crime.

Capital punishment is practiced in Maldives for serious crimes such as murder and drug trafficking. The Sharia law also allows for public flogging as a form of punishment, especially in cases of sex outside of marriage. This sentence is carried out more frequently on women than on men.

MALDIVES AND THE WORLD

Maldives has diplomatic relations with more than 50 countries and is a member of numerous international organizations, including the United Nations and the British Commonwealth. Through former president Gayoom, the country has been very active in the nonaligned movement and strongly supports the demilitarization of the Indian Ocean. An instance of the Maldivian government's strong desire for peace was its refusal to rent the former British air base on Gan to the Soviet Union for $1 million in 1977. For one of the least developed countries in the world, it was a strong demonstration of political willpower. As an Islamic state, Maldives is also very close to Arab nations and is a member of the Organization of the Islamic Conference.

It is in the South Asian Association for Regional Cooperation (SAARC) and the Alliance of Small Island States (AOSIS) that Maldives has made its mark. Set up in 1985 the seven-member SAARC aims to boost trade among member countries and to offer a unified front in the face of foreign intervention. Maldives chaired the leaders' summit several times. Among the proposals put forward by the country were the need to pay more attention to the children of SAARC countries and the designation of 1992 as the "SAARC Year of the Environment." Maldives also did much to defuse tensions between member countries India and Pakistan whenever relations between the two neighbors hit a low.

Being at the forefront of the battle against global warming, Maldives was instrumental in setting up AOSIS in 1992. It was after a conference in Male on the rise in sea levels that the organization came into being. A grouping of 42 small island states in Asia, the Pacific, the Atlantic Ocean, and the Caribbean Sea, the alliance concentrates on climatic change and other environmental issues. Maldives speaks on behalf of small island states in the international arena.

ECONOMY

A Maldivian fisherman carrying his fresh catch to the main fish market in Male.

ALTHOUGH IT WAS ONE OF THE 20 poorest countries in the world 30 years ago, Maldives is now classified as a lower-middle-income country by the World Bank. In the year 2000 the country was taken off the list of least developed countries by the UN Development Program. For a country with almost no natural resources, this was quite an achievement.

Despite the slump in the world economy, Maldives was able to record an average 6.3 percent growth over the last 5 years. This success was due to sound economic policies and financial aid from the United Nations, the World Bank, and developed countries such as Japan and the oil-rich Arab states. In 2009, however, when the Nasheed government took control, it had to admit that the country was in the midst of a recession.

Traditionally Maldivians made a living from fishing and subsistence agriculture; today it is tourism that brings in more revenue. Maldives has also embarked on a light industrialization program.

FISHING

Until the early 1970s the major economic activity was fishing. The fisheries industry is still the second source of foreign exchange and accounts for half of all exports. This sector employs 11 percent of the labor force and traditionally contributes about 7 percent of GDP, generating annual revenues of $100 million. Maldives claims a 200-mile

Maldives has one of the highest gross domestic products in South Asia. However, income disparity is marked, with islanders in the remote atolls living just above the poverty line. The contrast between the super-luxurious tourist resorts and the villages that are scratching a living out of poor sandy soil is almost indecent.

Fishermen using rods to catch tuna.

(322-km) exclusive economic zone, so the country has an enormous supply of fish. Every man in Maldives has engaged in fishing at one time or another, even if it is just to catch the day's meal. Those who are in between jobs know that they can always fall back on fishing to make a living.

Fishing in Maldives is still carried on in the traditional manner, using rod or lines and hooks. Nets are never used because they are ecologically more damaging to marine life. For this reason Maldivian fish exports are certified dolphin-safe. The catch is mostly skipjack tuna, but yellow fin tuna, little tuna, mackerel, and sharks are also caught. Islanders go out to sea in the early morning, immediately after dawn prayers. A crew of eight or nine takes their place in the boat, and they do not have to go very far to get their catch.

FISH PROCESSING

Most of the fish are processed before being exported to Europe and Asia. The best fish are chilled and are flown immediately to Japan to be made into sashimi. The rest are frozen, canned, salted, or smoked. Fish for freezing and canning are taken to the processing plant on Felivaru in Lhaviyani Atoll. Salting and smoking are carried out on a few uninhabited islands. The fish are gutted at night, when the sun is down. They are then placed into containers of salt to be preserved. After they have absorbed the salt, they are laid out to dry in the sun. "Maldive fish," which is very popular in the islands and in Sri Lanka, is a unique product of Maldives. After the fish has been gutted and filleted, it is boiled in salted water. The boiled fish is then smoked above a wood fire. To preserve it further, it is left to dry in the sun. "Maldive fish" keeps well for a very long period.

Fishermen's Day on December 10 highlights the importance of fishing in the country. This festival celebrates the contribution of fishermen to the economy.

TOURISM

Tourism in Maldives started in earnest in 1972 with the opening of the first resort on Kurumba Island. Recognizing its potential, the Maldivian government was quick to tap into this new source of income and embarked on an ambitious plan to develop the archipelago into a top luxury tourist destination. Tourists come to Maldives to dive among the impressive marine life and relax on the beautiful beaches. Most of them are Europeans, but Asians are coming in greater numbers. Tourism is the top foreign exchange earner, bringing in about $500 million a year. The tourist industry and related services contribute 28 percent of GDP and account for 90 percent of government tax revenue.

Maldivian tourism policy aims to offer guests quality accommodation and services in order to generate maximum revenue. To protect the local population's Muslim culture, tourists are isolated in their resorts. They also do not have much contact with local people. This sense of isolation is actually one of the reasons that 600,000 tourists are drawn to Maldives every year.

Tourism contributes a substantial amount of foreign currency to the country.

Tourist resorts are built only on uninhabited islands, but since 2009 tourists can visit villages on inhabited islands, thanks to a system of ferries linking more than 300 islands. In this way the government hopes to allow the revenues generated by tourism to trickle down to the locals. More than 90 resorts are operational, with another 65 under construction. The older resorts are located in Male Atoll, but as demand rises, other islands in the central atolls have been given over to tourism.

Resort operators lease the island from the government, but they have to follow the strict Tourism Law concerning environmental standards. For example they need a permit to cut down trees during the construction of the hotel and are not allowed to import water from any of the inhabited islands. The Maldives Association of Tourism Industry is a private-sector organization of resort owners, tour agencies, and diving schools. It maps out policies and helps promote tourism in the country.

The 2004 Indian Ocean tsunami dealt a heavy blow to Maldives tourism, inflicting damages of $375 million. Moreover many resorts were damaged and had to close down for renovations or rebuilding. Resort damages came up to $100 million, which was mainly covered by private insurance. However, the tourism industry bounced back quite fast and, within a year, the resorts were doing good business again.

AGRICULTURE

Maldivian soil is very poor, and only about 10 percent of the total land area is suitable for agriculture. To meet the growing demands of the population, large quantities of fresh vegetables, fruit, and meat must be imported, especially for the tourist industry. The government actively encourages the agricultural sector to prevent a drain of much-needed foreign reserves.

Large-scale agriculture is carried out on more than 941 uninhabited islands leased from the government. Because the islands have no natural source of water, such as rivers or lakes, the growing of crops depends on natural rainfall during the southwest monsoon. Maldivian planters use mainly organic fertilizers and rotate their crops for a better yield.

Despite the limitations, the agricultural sector still manages to produce a number of cash crops. The most bountiful is the coconut, and its production remains the dominant agricultural activity. Coconuts are eaten and can be used to make a variety of products from soap to rope. Other food crops include breadfruit, root vegetables, and fruits. Islanders in the southern atolls continue to cultivate and consume taro, cassava, and sweet potatoes. The cultivation of millet and maize has almost disappeared, as Maldivians today rely more heavily on rice as a staple food.

Maldivians collecting water for agriculture. Maldives does not have natural sources of water.

THE MALDIVIAN CURRENCY

The rufiyaa (Rf) is the unit of money used in Maldives. It is divided into 100 laari. Bank notes come in denominations of 5, 10, 20, 50, 100, and 500 rufiyaa. Very pretty and colorful, they feature objects that are typically Maldivian, such as coconuts or fishing boats. Coins in circulation are 1, 2, 5, 10, 25, and 50 laari, and 1 and 2 rufiyaa. The first four have dimpled edges. The rufiyaa became the national currency in 1981. Coins were first minted in the late 16th century, but they were shaped like hairpins and were not round.

With easy access to the sea, Maldives was a veritable mint when cowry shells were used as the unit of currency by the countries in the Indian Ocean. The islanders devised a way of collecting them by placing palm fronds in the shallow waters. When the fronds were laden with cowries, they were pulled onto the beach, where the cowries were left to die in the sun. The shells were then buried in the sand so that the animals decomposed underground, leaving only the shiny shells.

Many women tend a vegetable garden to grow some food for the family. They also keep some chickens for meat and eggs as well as a goat for milk.

INDUSTRY

The industrial sector includes traditional occupations and modern industry. Traditional occupations, such as boat building, weaving, rope making, and handicraft making, have received a new lease on life with the advent of tourism. This sector employs about a fifth of the labor force, mainly women, since the products are made by hand. Modern industry includes fish canning, garment manufacturing, and the making of PVC pipes.

The industrial sector accounts for less than 7 percent of the GDP. The Maldivian government is aware that this sector must grow in order to meet the demands of the economy. However, the small size of the domestic market, lack of infrastructure, shortage of skilled workers, and lack of raw materials pose serious problems to the development of this sector.

The traditional boat of Maldives is the caravel-styled dhoni (DOE-nih). Almost every family in the islands owns a small dhoni. With its distinctive tall, curved prow, it is strong and built to last. Equipped with a diesel engine, the long and slender boat has a fabric roof, a wooden bench running down each side, and a sail as a backup. The helmsman uses his legs to steer the vessel. He sits or stands on the flat stern, holding the tiller with his foot and trolling a fishing line. Dhoni come in all sizes and are used for fishing as well as for transportation. An odi (O-di-h) is a large dhoni used for cargo.

The basic design of the dhoni has hardly changed over the centuries. The best dhoni are built in Raa Atoll by master craftsmen who pass on their skill from generation to generation. These builders command a lot of respect as well as high salaries. They do not need to draw building plans, and the construction can take a few months because the carpenter uses only his hands and a few tools. Dhoni are traditionally made of coconut wood in a thatched hut at the water's edge. The hull is constructed from planks of hardwood taken from the base of the tree and fitted together with wooden nails like a precise jigsaw puzzle. The whole boat is secured with copper nails and wooden pegs. Once completed, the dhoni is painted all over with fish oil to preserve the wood and ease its launch into the water.

Workmen unloading bags of sand imported from India that Maldives needs for its construction industry.

TRADE

Maldives imports much more than it exports. All imports in 2008 totaled $1.276 billion and consisted mainly of petroleum products, ships, machinery, and consumer goods, including food. In the same year the country exported $113 million worth of goods. Marine exports accounted for most of all exports, the major items being frozen and dried skipjack tuna. Other exports included clothing and scrap metal.

Singapore supplies Maldives with more than a quarter of all imported goods. Not all of the products originate in Singapore, which is a very convenient consignment place and where suppliers offer favorable credit. Sri Lanka is another important trading partner, both providing imports and absorbing exports. Thailand is the biggest market for Maldivian products, buying up about a third of all exports. The United Kingdom, with which Maldives has retained excellent relations, is another important export partner.

TRANSPORTATION AND COMMUNICATION

Most islands are so small that the inhabitants go everywhere on foot or by bicycle. Nevertheless cars, including taxis, do exist, especially on Male, where the vehicle is viewed as a status symbol. The love affair of the Maldivian with everything motorized, including cars and motorcycles, continues unabated, and the streets of Male are often jammed with expensive imported sports cars. To travel from one island to another, Maldivians use speedboats or ferries. The national airline, Maldivian, flies to India and Sri Lanka, and also operates domestic flights to the five airports in the islands. Most tourists arrive in Male by charter flights and transfer to a seaplane, helicopter, or speedboat for the trip to the resort.

The people of Male and the resort islands have easy access to telephones, fax service, and the Internet. Phone ownership is high on Male. The telecommunications network covers the whole archipelago, and all inhabited islands and all resorts are connected by telephone and fax services. Mobile phone subscriptions are growing at a fast rate.

A Maldivian air taxi, parked in the waters off a resort.

ENVIRONMENT

The crystalline waters of Maldives.

CHAPTER 5

BY ALL ACCOUNTS the preservation of the environment is one of the most pressing problems in Maldives. Population pressures and economic development have led to a degradation of living conditions, including the erosion of the shoreline on most islands and the depletion of the natural aquifer (underground water table).

In addition, the disposal of waste by both private individuals and corporate entities such as tourist resorts is cause for concern.

A garbage dump and recycling area on Hitaddu Island.

Maldives is finding enormous difficulty in preserving its pristine environment. On the one hand it is this pristine environment that attracts tourists to the country, making it Maldives's only economic asset. On the other hand the very presence of these tourists is leading to the destruction of many ecosystems.

It is a well-known fact that Maldives is threatened by global warming and the rise in sea levels. With no island higher than 8.2 feet (2.5 m), the archipelago runs a definite risk of being submerged by the seas. Former president Gayoom started the drum beat in the 1980s when he highlighted the danger faced by the Maldives to the rest of the world. His successor, Nasheed, has made the environment the top priority of his government since coming to power in late 2008. In 2009 *Time* magazine proclaimed Nasheed a "Hero of the Environment."

EROSION

A quarter of the 200 inhabited islands suffer from coastal erosion. This happens when the sand surrounding the island is washed away by the sea. The sandy soil of the whole island gets looser, threatening buildings and livelihoods. The traditional building materials in Maldives are coral and sand. To make walls, most islanders collect the pieces of coral from the sea and stick them together with quicklime (melted coral). The depletion of coral in the waters off the inhabited islands causes the sea waves to wash to the shore with more force since there is nothing to slow them down. The undertow carries away the loose sand, causing the shoreline to recede. Global warming as well as the dumping of wastes into the sea also contributes to the death of corals. Tidal surges are a fortnightly occurrence on some islands, flooding low-lying houses.

In 1987 and 1991 large areas of Male flooded as storm waves pounded the island. As a result, sea defenses were built all around the island with

Coastal vegetation along the beach of Rangali Island. Erosion of the sand has left the roots of the vegetation exposed.

the aid of the Japanese government. These came in the form of tetrapods, concrete blocks with four fat legs, each approximately 3.3 feet (1 m) long. These blocks can be stacked in rows and layers so that they interlock to form a tall wall. The 9.9-foot-high (3-m-high) wall took 14 years to build. Because the tetrapod breakwater has gaps, it allows seawater to pass through while absorbing the force of the waves. Built at a cost of $21 million per mile, it did not come cheap.

Attempts at land reclamation have all failed because the reclaimed area keeps getting washed away. Sea walls also are eventually destroyed by the waves. As for the gabions put in place by some resort islands, they rust and fall apart after a few years.

THE NATURAL ENVIRONMENT

Since the Maldivian atolls are of coralline origin, most of the islands have sandy soil that does not support much variety in vegetation. In general the soil in the center of the island is usually rich while the coastal areas are less fertile. The natural vegetation is tropical rain forest, which can be classified into five categories: beach pioneers, littoral hedge, sublittoral thicket, climax forest, and mangrove and swamp forests. About 20 species occur on the beach, and they are highly salt tolerant. The littoral hedge is made up of bushy shrubs such as *Scaevola sericea* (Hawaiian half-flower) and *Pemphis acidula* (*bantigi*). Numbering about 10 species, these grow many branches and are quite wide. Behind the beaches grows a distinct community of small flowering trees that are more salt-sensitive: hibiscus, elderflower, beach gardenia, kou. The climax forest, farther inland, is the most common vegetation in the islands. One of the largest varieties is the lantern tree, which can grow up to 65.5 feet (20 m) in height. The sea almond tree is another regular feature of Maldivian vegetation. Mangroves, of which 13 species have been recorded, are most extensive in the southern atolls. They are usually found on the ocean side of the islands.

Terrestrial animals are limited in Maldives and very few species are endemic (occurring only in Maldives). Native land mammals include the fruit

"The Maldives faces daunting environmental risks that threaten to undermine its economic achievements." —Richard Damania, senior environmental economist

The greatest threat to Maldives in the next few decades comes from global warming. As industrialized nations emit more noxious gases into the atmosphere, the Earth warms up in what is called the "greenhouse effect." This leads polar ice caps to melt and sea levels to rise. Even a slight rise will be catastrophic for Maldives since most of the islands are less than 7 feet (2 m) in height. In addition most islands are cup-shaped with a low center.

Scientists predict that sea levels could rise by as much as 15 inches (38 cm) in the next few decades. The slightest storm could wash away some of the low islands. Some islands, such as Male, are already sinking. Even if the islands do not actually sink, they have become more vulnerable to climatic conditions such as El Niño. More frequent storms have been observed in the Indian Ocean, and surging tides pose a definite threat to the islands.

Optimists think that Maldives will not sink because the coral reefs surrounding the archipelago are constantly growing so that the islands will rise as sea levels rise. However, the reefs are not growing as fast as the sea is rising, and it is feared that the whole archipelago will be completely submerged in the next century.

Unfortunately for the Maldivians, there is nothing much that they can do on their own to stop global warming. It takes a concerted effort from the world's industrialized nations to change their habits and switch to more ecologically friendly methods of production. In the worst-case scenario, the whole population will have to relocate elsewhere, and government officials are seriously considering the option of buying an island or piece of land in India, Sri Lanka, or even in Australia.

bat, two species of flying fox, and the garden shrew. They are quite widely distributed throughout the islands. Reptiles and amphibians are slightly more plentiful, with two geckos, two lizards, two snakes, the snake skink, a short-headed frog, and a large toad. Five types of turtles nest in the Maldives, which is an important nesting site for the green turtle. More than 100 species of birds have also been recorded, mainly seabirds.

The marine environment is much more varied, with the reefs supporting a host of wildlife. The reefs themselves are made of coral, of which more than 250 species have been recorded in Maldivian waters. The most common species is the acropora, and it can take any number of forms, ranging from flat plates to round brain-like structures. The reefs are home to fish, shellfish, sponges, mollusks, starfish, sea urchins, and worms. Around 700 species of reef fish swim about the lagoons and on the coral reefs. Marine mammals living in the open sea around the archipelago include seven species of dolphins and nine species of whales.

The beautiful coral reefs of Maldives teem with life and color.

"We do not want to leave the Maldives, but we also do not want to be climate refugees living in tents for decades."
—President Mohamed Nasheed

ENDANGERED SPECIES

Of the native terrestrial animal species, *Pteropus hypomelanus maris*, a subspecies of the giant fruit bat, is considered to be endangered due to excessive culling. Because it is not widely distributed, its numbers are declining. The white tern is limited to Addu Atoll, and it is the only protected bird species in Maldives.

It is underwater that more species are threatened. Coral, the very backbone of the marine ecosystem, is a very fragile creature that is susceptible to the slightest change in environment. Coral dies when the water temperature changes or when the mineral content is affected by the dumping of wastes. Aquatic mammals that are at risk are the dugong and some species of dolphin. Classified as vulnerable by the International Union for Conservation of Nature, the whale shark is the largest fish in the world. It makes its home year-round in Maldives, the only such occurrence in the Indian Ocean. All four species of sea turtles that nest in Maldives are considered most endangered. The leatherback, which is an occasional visitor, is rare. Turtles are hunted by the locals for food, and their eggs are considered a delicacy.

A whale shark swimming in the waters just off Ari Atoll.

NATURAL DISASTERS

The most sensational natural disaster to hit the Maldivian archipelago was the December 2004 Indian Ocean tsunami, one of the deadliest in history. Following a strong earthquake off the coast of Indonesia, many communities in several countries bordering the Indian Ocean were destroyed by waves 100 feet (30 m) high. In Maldives more than 100 people lost their lives, 21 islands were destroyed, and 11,000 people were made homeless. Only nine islands were reported to have escaped any flooding. A large portion of Male was flooded, and many inhabited islands were completely submerged at the peak of the tsunami. Some low-lying islands have literally disappeared. Despite the loss of life and damage to infrastructure, much more harm could have come to the islands if not for the deep inter-atoll channels that absorbed much of the strength of the wave. Male's tetrapod wall also lessened the brunt of the tsunami, and mangrove-fringed islands were better protected. Although the damaged tourist resorts were repaired and opened for business within one year of the disaster, the effects are still being felt among the Maldivian population.

In May 1998 an unusually strong El Niño led to the destruction of large areas of coral reef. For about two weeks, surface water temperatures rose above 90 °F (32 °C), resulting in the loss of the algae that live within the coral polyps. These are the algae that give the coral its color and provide nourishment for it. More than 90 percent of animals with algae covering, including corals, giant clams, anemones, and soft corals, showed heavy bleaching to depths of 60 feet (20 m). When the coral dies, it becomes brittle and is broken up by the wave actions. Some of the coral that died may have been hundreds of years old, and it will take decades for the reefs to recover.

Several projects are under way to rescue the threatened species. The Maldives Whale Shark Research Program (MWSRP) was set up in 2006 by an international team of marine biologists to research into the demography and movements of the whale shark population in Maldives. Their overall objectives are to educate the public on the animal and to protect and conserve the species. The MWSRP is collaborating with the ministry of environment to develop the South Ari Marine Protected Area dedicated to sharks. Turtle rescue and nesting projects are carried out by resorts on an individual basis. Various organizations are also involved in coral regeneration.

ECOTOURISM

The tourism industry depends on the fragile ecosystem of the islands and reefs for its survival. To preserve this source of revenue, tourist developments are governed by a set of rules and regulations. Holiday resorts are built only on uninhabited islands so that the contact between Maldivians and foreigners is kept to a minimum, thus preserving the traditional way of life.

The Tourism Act spells out detailed regulations on the building and maintenance of resorts. Construction of permanent structures is limited to 20 percent of the total land area of the island, and the buildings cannot be more than two stories high. They must be at least 15 feet (5 m) from the shoreline. No large or rare tree can be cut to make way for a building, and each tree that is cut down must be replaced by the planting of two other trees on the same island. Resorts are also autonomous in waste management and water supply. Each island is fitted with a desalination plant for water as well as with incinerators, compactors, and bottle crushers for disposal of waste. Open burning of trash and dumping of sewage in the ocean is strictly prohibited.

On their side resorts have come up with recycling programs such as composting of kitchen waste or the production of charcoal from waste wood. Many have installed solar panels to tap into this renewable source of energy and one resort is even experimenting with using cold sea water from 984 feet (300 m) deep to cool air-conditioning fan coils. They are also very active in the educational field. Most resorts employ marine biologists to educate their guests on the marine ecosystem and to conduct research on marine species and to take part in conservation projects, such as coral propagation, turtle nesting, and shark tracking.

Tourists are exhorted to be ecologically conscious by making the right choices—for example, by drinking desalinated water instead of asking for imported bottled water. Many tour groups also ask their members to take their nonbiodegradable waste back to their home countries where disposal facilities are available.

All resorts tag themselves as being ecofriendly but in actual fact, it is very difficult to be ecologically neutral in this industry. Most claims are just marketing savvy.

GOVERNMENT MEASURES

One of the first decisions of President Nasheed when he took office was to announce that the country would become carbon-neutral by the year 2020 in a bid to slow down the effect of climate change on Maldives and also to prompt the rest of the world into action to prevent environmental disasters. To achieve this objective, individuals and corporations will switch to renewable energy sources where possible, and the country will balance the carbon that it emits through measures such as planting trees elsewhere. The government is also levying a "green" tax of one dollar a day per tourist, which will go to fund climate change projects in the republic. Eventually, it will also provide the capital for the purchase of land in case the population has to move out.

Although there are no national parks in Maldives, the government has set aside 25 sites as Protected Marine Areas. These are scattered over the archipelago but most of them can be found in Male Atoll (10) and Alifu (6) and are usually popular diving sites. The following activities are prohibited within the PMAs: anchoring (except in an emergency), coral and sand mining, rubbish dumping, removal of any natural object or living creatures, fishing of any kind with exception of traditional live-bait fishing, and any other activity that may cause damage to the area or its marine life. In addition, shark fishing is banned as well as the hunting of turtles and their eggs.

MALDIVIANS

A Maldivian boy in front of a coral wall in Meedhu.

A N OFFICIAL ESTIMATE IN JULY 2009 put the population of Maldives at 396,334. Although this figure seems low in absolute terms, Maldives is classified as the 11th most densely populated country in the world.

Although Maldives still has a young population, growth has slowed down in recent years, with adolescents accounting for slightly more than a quarter of the total. Life expectancy is 72 years for men and 76 years for women. Women form about 49 percent of the population.

An elderly man cycling. Life expectancy for Maldivians has lengethened over the years.

In their language Maldivians call themselves "Dhivehi," which is derived from a Sanskrit word that means "Letters of Island People." About 10,000 Dhivehi live on Minicoy, an island under Indian administration. Maldives also plays host to 80,000 expatriate workers, some of whom reside illegally in the archipelago.

More than one-third of the Maldivians live in Male, which is experiencing such severe overcrowding that it has embarked on a land reclamation program. To relieve population pressure on the capital, the man-made island of Hulhumale is being developed to house government offices, industrial areas, shopping centers as well as residential estates. In the other inhabited islands, the population is spread out quite unevenly. The larger islands, especially those that have easy access to good fishing, are more popular, with as many as 3,000 persons on one island. In general each island is home to between 200 and 800 people.

A MELTING POT

Maldivians say that the earliest inhabitants of their country were the Redins, the builders of the archaeological ruins found on some of the islands. Tall and big, the Redins had brown hair and light skin. Their faces were long, and they had blue eyes. Norwegian ethnologist and author Thor Heyerdahl speculated that they worshiped the sun, in the same way that pre-Columbian

Maldivian boys playing in the water. Most Maldivians closely resemble Indians and Sri Lankans in physical appearance.

One of the striking aspects of the Maldivian character is the lack of obvious emotion. Maldivians are a quiet people who are not given to expressive demonstrations. Children are taught to keep their thoughts and feelings to themselves, even within the family. Thus they do not appear to be close to one another, especially to their fathers. When Maldivians meet their friends, they do not seem to be particularly happy. The Maldivian language has no words for "hello" and "thank you," and there are very few expressions of concern. Maldivians take time to warm up to strangers, although they show the utmost courtesy at all times.

There is a large element of stoic resignation in the Maldivian approach to life. Surrounded by the sea and sometimes living at the mercy of the elements, they take nothing for granted. Maldivians are a peaceful people who do not relish confrontation.

people in South America did. The mystery of the Redins will probably never be solved, since none of today's Maldivians can trace their ancestry back to them.

The people of Maldives present a melting pot of ethnic influences. Most of them are dark-skinned and have straight black hair and black eyes. They are attractive and are not very tall. In physical appearance they are closer to Indians and Sri Lankans. The fairer ones may be descended from the Portuguese who occupied the islands in the 16th century. The Maldivians also have traces of Arab and African blood. Maldivians swear that they can tell which island people come from by the way they walk.

ETHNIC COMMUNITIES

The Giraavaru people claim to be the aboriginal inhabitants of Maldives. Descended from the Tamils of South India, they are indistinguishable from the rest of the population in physical appearance. However, they have always kept to themselves and maintained a separate identity. The Giraavaru follow different customs and speak with a different accent. The women tie their

The survival of the Giraavaru as a distinct community is in danger because many young people marry other Maldivians and get absorbed into the mainstream society. There are fewer than 150 Giraavaru today.

hair in a bun on the right side of the head instead of the usual practice of tying it on the left side. After their island was badly affected by soil erosion, the Giraavaru were moved by the government to the island of Hulhule in 1968. They later resettled in the western quarter of Male when the airport was expanded.

The descendants of Indian traders who came to Maldives in the 19th century make up a distinct ethnic and religious minority. Numbering a few hundred, they are Muslims. A number of Sri Lankans have also settled in Maldives, mainly to work in the bars in resort hotels because the Muslim locals do not touch alcohol.

THE SOUTHERN MINORITY

Physically separated from the rest of Maldives by the deep One-and-a-Half-Degree Channel, the people of the southernmost atolls have long felt distinct from Male. They speak their own dialect, which is more related to early Sinhalese, the language of Sri Lanka, than to Dhivehi, the language of Maldives. Most Maldivians do not understand the southern dialect. The southerners also once had direct trade links with Sri Lanka.

Underlying tensions between the south and Male came to a peak in the 1950s and 1960s when the government stopped the southerners from selling their "Maldive fish" directly to Sri Lankan traders. Islanders were also forbidden from being employed by the British military base that had just been set up on Gan. In 1959, under the leadership of Abdulla Afif Didi, the three southern atolls joined the United Suvadive Islands and broke away from Male. They formed a People's Council, elected Didi as president, and established a trading corporation and a bank. The rebellion was short-lived, because the Maldivian government sent armed troops in 1962 to bring the southerners to heel. The soldiers destroyed all the homes on Thinadhoo, the capital of Huvadhoo Atoll, forcing the people to flee to neighboring islands. They did not return until four years later. Didi fled to the Seychelles, but he is still talked about on his home island of Hithadhoo.

Young girls from the Southern atolls of the Maldives.

Today the Maldivian government encourages the development of the southern atolls. The country's second international airport was opened on Gan, and resort developments are on the way. A causeway connects the island to three other islands in the vicinity, making Gan a center for tourism.

WOMEN

Women in Maldives have equal rights under the law. They can run for office, manage a business, and own land and houses. Although women cannot be judges or priests, they have access to equal educational and employment opportunities. The Ministry of Health and Family, run by the only female minister, looks after the development of women.

Maldivian women enjoy equal rights under the nation's constitution.

Women lead an active economic and social life. In the evening, island women like to meet on their verandas and have a good chat. In Male, groups of women like to go for a stroll in the evening.

Married women enjoy a certain amount of independence. They can retain their maiden names and exercise much control over family matters. They can acquire land or property. About one-third of the houses and coconut trees in the islands belong to women. In most villages women are the heads of the household because the men go to work in the resorts or are out fishing all day. An inheritance is split among all the children, regardless of gender.

FAMILY LIFE

The family forms the basis of Maldivian society. About 80 percent of Maldivian households are nuclear families composed of a married couple and their children rather than an extended family. The extended family, however, lives within the same compound and helps look after the children. It is usually the mother's family that is assigned this task. Maldivian families tend to be large, with an average of five children. Birth control is only available to married couples, and the declining fertility rate in the last few years bears testimony to its success. Children live with their parents until they get married and set up their own household.

Families wake up very early to say their morning prayers, between 4:30 and 5:00 A.M. Fishermen get ready for the day and set off before sunrise. Women prepare breakfast, clean the house, and get the children ready for school. All outdoor work is carried out by the men while women are in charge of all household chores.

The family meets twice a day for meals. When they are together, they say very little to one another and rarely express any emotion. People talk very softly, even to the children. Few children speak to their fathers.

A grandfather with his grandchildren.

SOCIAL STRUCTURE

Maldives practiced the caste system well into the 1920s. Although the castes have been abolished, Maldivians still put a lot of emphasis on social classes and wealth. Traditionally there was a significant gap between the elite in Male and the population of the other islands. This gap is slowly closing with the government's policy of raising the standard of living in the outer islands. Nevertheless the influential families in Male, such as the Kaloa, Fulu, Maniku, and Didi, who used to be very close to the sultan, still control the government and business sectors. They also furnish the country's religious leaders, professionals, and scholars.

In the islands the atoll chief, island chief, and religious magistrate are the most important people. The boat owner is also at the top of the social structure. He employs all the fishermen. Next on the social ladder are the boat builders and the medicine men. Skilled craftsmen also command a lot of respect. At the bottom of the ladder is the toddy tapper. He looks after the coconuts, and taps their sap to make syrup and the toddy drink.

LIFESTYLE

Motorcycles and bicycles are the most common mode of transportation in Maldives.

DESPITE THE DEVELOPMENT OF tourism, not much has changed in the Maldivian style of life. Daily activities revolve around Islam and religious observances. The government has certainly brought vast improvements to the life of islanders, but their lifestyle is still very much defined by the sea. Fishing and fish-related activities are their main concerns.

Male, however, has experienced enormous changes in the past 20 years. Land reclamation has enlarged the island, tall buildings have

Tuna fishermen at work. The sea is an integral part of Maldivian life.

A wide chasm exists between the lifestyle of Male and the outer islands. In the capital residents have to put up with overcrowding, noise pollution, and a fast-paced lifestyle. Villagers, on the other hand, have to make do with fewer conveniences, but they lead a much simpler lifestyle punctuated by visits with neighbors and communal activities.

replaced the one-story coral houses, and modern telecommunications have brought the rest of the world to Maldives. Thus young people from the islands look at Male as the epitome of modernity. They come here for education or for work. To the islander, it is in Male that one can acquire great wealth and enjoy the comforts of modern life.

VILLAGE LIFE

Villages are laid out on a rectangular plan, with each family leasing an area of 49 feet (15 m) by 98 feet (30 m) from the government. The main house is in the center of the compound and is used for sleeping. The kitchen and bathroom are separate structures within the compound. Maldivian bathrooms do not have roofs. By tradition someone climbing a coconut tree near a house is supposed to shout to announce his presence to those using the open-air bathroom. Houses are made of coral or thatched palm fronds. Families spend much of their time in the shade of trees in the garden or on the veranda.

A Maldivian woman cooking in the kitchen of her village home.

MARRIAGE AND DIVORCE

Maldivians marry early, the legal age being 18. Most newly married couples are between 20 and 24 years old. Maldivians also marry often. There is no stigma attached to a woman who has been married before, and it is common for some men to have had 20 wives.

Although some modern couples in Male choose to get married in Western dress and throw a party for their guests, most people keep their weddings simple. The ceremony, celebrated by the local judge or ghaazee, takes place in the groom's house or the island office. Present are the groom, his father, the bride's uncle, and two witnesses. Prior to the ceremony, the groom has received the consent of the bride and her father. The man must pay his wife a "bride price," but the woman does not have to bring a dowry. After marriage, the couple usually lives with the wife's parents.

According to Islam, a man may have up to four wives at a time if he can afford it and if he treats them all equally, but a woman cannot be married to more than one man at a time. Most Maldivian men, however, cannot afford to keep more than one wife. The wealthier fishermen or traveling boatmen may have wives on several islands. Most people get married because sex outside marriage is illegal, and adultery is a serious crime.

The Family Law introduced in 2001 made divorce much less easy than it used to be. Whereas once a man could divorce his wife simply by telling her that he was divorcing her, unilateral divorce is now illegal. Both parties have to go through the courts, as in most Western countries, and a divorce is only granted when all attempts at reconciliation have failed. The strict measures initially led to a decline in the number of divorces, but rates have been rising again since 2006, and the Maldives still has one of the highest divorce rates in the world. More alarming is the fact that men have reverted to the Islamic custom, considering divorce as their unalienable "right."

Although it is traditional for Maldivians to marry and divorce often, the government is urging the population not to be too hasty in dissolving their marriages. This is to prevent the disintegration of families and family values.

A water well near a village house in the Male Atoll.

The village square is a platform of logs located on the beach or in a central location near the sea. It is constructed in the shade of a large tree. The men of the village come to the square to relax, play cards or chess, or sleep. Because everybody comes to the square at some time or other, important notices are posted on the trunk of the tree.

Apart from a field where young men and boys play soccer, there are no other amenities for children. They play in the sea or on the beach. Adults, however, have a social club that looks after their welfare.

Villages are quiet and peaceful. They are virtually devoid of any male presence during the day because the men are out for fishing. Women and girls keep the sandy streets clean by sweeping them with a broom made from the spines of coconut leaves. Each woman is in charge of the public ground in front of her compound. A few times a week the village women get together to sweep the beach and other public areas.

Schoolchildren in uniform.

EDUCATION

Although education is not compulsory, most children do go to school. Enrollment in primary level has been 100 percent since 2002. The Maldivian education system is based on the British system, although the instruction is in Dhivehi (DEE-vay-hih), the local language, for the first few years. Today Maldives has a literacy rate of 96.3 percent, making it the most literate country in South Asia and in the Indian Ocean region.

Children start their education at the age of three in religious schools called *makthab* (MOK-tub). In the islands this may be under the shade of a tree on the beach or in a small room. Young children receive religious instruction and learn to read and write in Dhivehi and Arabic. At the age of six, they enroll in a primary school. Every atoll has at least one government primary school. Standards are high, and students are expected to read and write in Dhivehi, English, and Arabic by the age of seven. Secondary school starts in the sixth grade when the children are 10 years old and ends with 10th grade. Children

A young boy answering an arithmetic question in school. The introduction of broadband Internet has helped raise the standard of education and liven up school lessons for students.

learn Dhivehi, English, mathematics, science, fine arts, environmental studies, and calligraphy. Secondary education is available in all atoll capitals and on large islands. Those who wish to continue their studies must transfer to one of three higher secondary schools (one in Male, and one each in the far south and in the far north) for 11th and 12th grades and take the British GCE "A" level examination. The Maldives College of Higher Education in Male is the only postsecondary institution of learning with faculties of health, education, tourism, and engineering as well as Sharia law. Young people who want to attend college must go overseas, usually to Sri Lanka, India, Great Britain, or Australia. President Nasheed's government is planning on founding the country's first university. English is introduced as a second language in the first grade and is the medium of instruction in grades 9 and 10.

HEALTH CARE

Maldives has made such spectacular progress in health care that life expectancy has jumped by 26 years since 1980. Communicable diseases have

A doctor examines an X-ray of a young girl thought to be suffering from thalassemia, a genetic disease of the blood.

also been kept under control, with no cases of malaria reported in the past 15 years. The infant mortality rate was halved in 40 years.

The main hospital in Maldives is the Indira Gandhi Memorial Hospital in Male. The 275-bed facility provides a wide range of medical services with 15 areas of specialization. There is also a smaller private hospital in Male with facilities for surgery. There are another six regional hospitals located in the central, north, and south atolls as well as 45 smaller-scale health centers and 36 health posts serving the islands.

Basic health care is provided by the family health workers stationed on every inhabited island. Their job is to provide vaccinations to children and pregnant women, promote family planning, and control communicable diseases such as tuberculosis and viral epidemics. One vital aspect of their mission is to educate the island population about healthy practices and the importance of hygiene in their daily activities. For more serious medical treatment, islanders go to the atoll health center where there is at least one doctor.

Many Maldivians also consult a local medicine man or woman called a hakim. These traditional practitioners believe that good health depends on the balance between the hot, cold, dry, and wet properties of the body. Thus, when someone has a fever, the hakim recommends "cold" foods and herbal remedies. For the flu the patient has to eat dry fish. The hakim is treated with great respect in the island communities.

MALE DRESS

As an Islamic nation, Maldivians dress very conservatively. Although the tropical climate means that the weather is very hot, the Maldivian islanders do not like to expose their skin. Most men in Male wear trousers and a short-sleeved shirt. Office workers usually wear long-sleeved shirts with a tie. Fishermen and other village folks, given the nature of their work, prefer casual and comfortable attire. They usually wear a T-shirt over a sarong, a

Fishermen dressed in casual shirts and sarongs preparing to fish.

piece of cloth that is tied around the waist and reaches to the ankles. When they go into the sea, they hitch up the sarong to turn it into a loincloth.

FEMALE DRESS

Women in Male can be seen wearing Western dresses and even short skirts. The usual attire, however, is a brightly colored long-sleeved dress that reaches just below the knees. Like the village men, they also wear a sarong, but it is worn underneath the dress, like a petticoat. More fashionable women like to go out in a discreetly patterned dress that reaches the ankles and has long sleeves. It has a high waist and a distinctive wide collar embroidered with gold and silver thread. The embroidery takes weeks to complete. The dress is worn tight across the arms and chest and loose over the hips. Women complete the outfit with a headscarf that is pinned to the hair without covering it completely. The village women wear more conservative and casual clothes because their work requires them to be comfortably dressed.

A Maldivian woman wearing a patterned dress with an intricately embroidered collar.

WORKING HOURS

Maldivians start work early and end early. The working week is from Sunday to Thursday. Government officers start their day at 7:30 A.M. and finish it at 1:30 P.M. Many government workers have a second job in the afternoon to earn extra cash to make ends meet. Some senior officers operate resorts when they are off duty. The private sector starts later, between 8:30 and 9:00 A.M., but basically has the same number of working hours. Shops open before 9:00 A.M. and close between 9:00 and 11:00 P.M. All offices, shops, and eating places close for 15 minutes four times a day for prayers. Working hours are shortened during Ramadan, the Muslim fasting month.

RELIGION

A minaret of a mosque.

THE EARLIEST INHABITANTS OF Maldives were probably worshipers of the sun. Ruins that have been unearthed show places of worship facing the setting sun in the west. Today's Maldivians still retain some of these beliefs in their superstitions.

When settlers from India moved south to the islands, they brought with them their Hindu religion. Hinduism was later supplanted by Buddhism

A shop closed for prayers. Muslims are required to pray five times a day when possible.

Although the constitution grants freedom of religion to all Maldivians, it also states that only Sunni Muslims can enjoy the privilege of being Maldivian citizens. Fundamentalism is encroaching more and more into everyday life, with Sharia law being used more extensively. Islamic scholars and clerics are present in big numbers at the top rungs of government.

Maldivian girls studying the Koran.

brought by the Sri Lankans. However, with the arrival of Islam in the 12th century, both Hinduism and Buddhism disappeared completely. Maldivian children are taught the story of the conversion to show them how powerful their religion is. Today Islam is the only religion allowed in the country, and the country is 100 percent Sunni Muslim. Because the president is the guardian of the faith, according to the constitution, Islam pervades every aspect of life, and there is little distinction between the religious and the secular. In fact only Muslims are entitled to Maldivian citizenship.

THE ISLAMIC FAITH

Started in the seventh century by the Prophet Muhammad, Islam is the religion of most of the Arab world. It shares many common characteristics with Judaism and Christianity, the other two religions present in the region at that time. Called Muslims, followers of Islam believe in one single God (Allah) who is all-powerful. They also ascribe to all the Jewish and Christian

1. Shahadah (sha-hah-dah) is the declaration of the Islamic faith that "There is no God but Allah, and Muhammad is his prophet."

2. Salat (sah-LAT) or namadh (na-MAHD) is the call to prayer. All Muslims must pray five times a day facing Mecca. (Because some of the mosques in Maldives are built atop older structures that face the rising sun, the faithful sometimes have to say their prayers in a rather awkward position—for example, facing a corner, such as in the Friday Mosque in Male.)

3. Zakat (za-KAHT) is the act of giving charity to the needy.

4. Sawm, the practice of fasting. During this period, all Muslims must fast during the day.

5. Hajj is the pilgrimage to Mecca that should be done at least once in the lifetime of every Muslim.

A prayer tower with Koranic inscriptions on it.

prophets, but believe that it was Muhammad who received the word of Allah. Muslims do not ascribe any god-like qualities to Muhammad but revere him as the mouthpiece of Allah. Saying or doing anything against Islam is a serious crime in Maldives, and foreigners have been sentenced to jail or banishment for trying to promote other religions.

Born in Mecca in A.D. 570, Muhammad started having visions in the year 610. Claiming to act on the instructions of Allah, he launched a campaign against idolatry and injustice. The people of Mecca did not have any religion at that time. Muhammad soon gained a large following, especially among the poor and downtrodden, and he was persecuted by those in power. He managed to defeat his persecutors and imposed Islam throughout most of Arabia. With enormous zeal his followers spread the religion beyond the Middle East after his death.

RELIGIOUS PRACTICES

The teachings of Allah are set down in the Koran, which gives guidelines for every aspect of life. Muslims must read a page of the Koran every day of the year and adhere to its teachings strictly. Only unswerving faith and the right conduct will ensure that they will go to heaven after death. This is achieved by following the five pillars of Islam. Muslims must also abstain from consuming pork and alcohol, and cannot have contact with dogs. For this reason there are no dogs in Maldives.

Maldivians belong to the Sunni sect, the largest sect in Islam. Although their faith is strong, it is quite liberal. Maldivians follow the teachings of the Koran but have not adopted the more extreme practices of Muslims living under fundamentalist regimes. For example, women are not required to cover their faces with veils, although the burqa (long dress worn by Muslim women covering the whole body from head to toe) is becoming more common, and punishment does not always involve violent physical retribution.

A Maldivian woman in typical Islamic dress.

MALDIVIAN MOSQUES

Every island has a mosque for daily prayers, with separate sections for men and women. Male has more than 20 mosques, some of which are for women only. Most mosques are encircled by a peaceful garden with a well. Passersby help themselves to water from the well with long ladles. The oldest mosque in Maldives is the Friday Mosque, dating from 1656. It has a beautiful interior with superb carvings.

PRAYER TIMES

Maldivians pray five times a day facing northwest in the direction of Mecca. The first prayer session of the day is in the first hour before sunrise, the second at around noon, the third in mid-afternoon, the fourth at sunset, and the last prayer is in the early evening. Muslims know that they have to go to the mosque when they hear the call of the muezzin or mosque crier. In the old days the muezzin used to climb to the top of the minaret (a tower-like structure in the mosque) and shout out. Today mosques use a recording over loudspeakers on the minaret. The muezzin even appears on television. Shops and offices close for about 15 minutes after each call. Some people go to the mosque, while others spread out their prayer mats on the floor wherever they happen to be and kneel facing in the direction of Mecca.

THE ISLAMIC CALENDAR

Based on the cycles of the moon, the Islamic calendar started with the flight of Muhammad from Mecca in the year A.D. 622. That year is marked as year one of the Islamic calendar.

Shoes outside the Friday Mosque.

Each year is composed of 12 months: Muharram, Safar, Rabi I, Rabi II, Jumada I, Jumada II, Rajab, Sha'ban, Ramadan, Shawwal, Dhu'l-Qa'dah, and Dhu'l-Hijja. Because every month has only 30 days, the Islamic calendar moves faster than the Gregorian calendar that is used in most countries. It is for this reason that Muslim festivals and events do not fall on the same date every year. A new month starts on the evening when the new crescent moon is sighted.

The Friday Mosque.

All Maldivians refer to the Islamic calendar to mark personal events and dates. Those whose work deals with non-Muslims, however, also use the Gregorian calendar. In addition the islanders have devised their own calendar called *nakaly* (NAH-kah-lih). This calendar follows the changes in weather, and the rising and setting of the stars, the sun, and the moon. The year is divided into 28 two-week periods.

SUPERSTITIONS

Despite being staunch Muslims, Maldivians are also very superstitious people. They believe in a number of spirits that inhabit the sea, the sky, the trees, and the rain. These spirits are called *dhevi* (DAY-vi) in Dhivehi, or *jinnis* in Arabic. Although there are some helpful *dhevi*, most of them are malevolent. To keep them out Maldivians sleep with all the doors and windows tightly closed in spite of the heat. They also leave a kerosene lamp burning. Spirits help the islanders explain the forces of nature and any misfortune that befalls them. Maldivians do not see any conflict between their Islamic faith and their superstitions. Very often they recite verses from the Koran in an attempt to ward off evil spirits.

DHEVI

One historian has counted more than 170 different *dhevi*. Their spiritual leader is Buddevi, who lives in jungles, on the beach, near thick undergrowth, or around abandoned houses. Buddevi can take the shape of a cat or a man. It is said that anyone who sees it will fall sick. Another spirit, Odivaru Ressi, lives in the sea and harms fishermen, boats, and fish. The lord of death is called Vigani. He inhabits the seas and can be seen on the water near the horizon. Appearing sometimes like a small man or a monkey with thick hair, he uses an elephant-like trunk to suck food from the graves of the dead. Vigani is the cause of sudden death and epidemics.

Muslim graves.

The people of the island of Gadhdhoo, which is located in the southern end of Maldives, believe in murderous giant cats that once invaded the neighboring island of Gan and killed all the inhabitants. For this reason they consider Gan to be unlucky and use it only as an Islamic cemetery. Although Gadhdhoo is heavily populated, no family would ever dream of moving to Gan.

WITCH DOCTORS

To neutralize evil spirits, islanders appeal to the hakim, who is a witch doctor as well as a traditional medicine man. A combination of exorcist, conjurer, herbalist, and astrologer, the witch doctor is steeped in the art of *fandhita* (FAN-dih-tah). He becomes qualified to practice only after an arcane examination that is a mystery to most people. The witch doctor is most often called on when illness strikes, when a woman fails to conceive, or when the fishing catch is poor. He uses spells and lotions to cast out evil spirits. One remedy is to write phrases from the Koran on small strips of paper and stick them on the patient while reciting the sayings out loud.

A believer dresses in a costume woven with leaves to celebrate a religious occasion.

Witch doctors cast spells mainly to heal or to encourage the elements to behave more favorably, like providing a better catch to fishermen. Other forms of good magic include making a sacred vow to perform good deeds if a wish is fulfilled. This may involve a sacrifice or the giving of alms. When a child is sick, bananas or a special pancake are distributed to neighbors and friends. The amount of food to be distributed must be equal to the weight of the child. Black magic is also performed but very infrequently, and its practice may attract heavy punishment.

LANGUAGE

A man using the telephone. Most Maldivians
are bilingual in both Dhivehi and English.

THE OFFICIAL LANGUAGE OF Maldives is Dhivehi, a language that is unique to Maldives. Dhivehi is similar to other languages of the Indian subcontinent, but is not based on any one of them.

Many Maldivians also speak English, as it is an international business language and also because the country used to be a British protectorate. English is the medium of instruction in grades 9 to 10 because students take the same qualifying exams as British schoolchildren. As tourism is becoming an increasingly important sector of the economy now, more

English is the language of instruction in schools.

For a long time freedom of expression was nothing but an empty phrase, and the slightest criticism of the government could lead to banishment from Male to a distant island. Newspapers exercised self-censorship so as to retain their business license. Now the government wants to deregulate the media by inviting foreign investors.

A young girl reading the Koran. Many Maldivian children learn Arabic in order to read the Koran.

Maldivians are learning English so that they can work in tourism-related businesses, which are paying relatively higher wages.

In addition to the two languages Dhivehi and English, Maldivian children also learn Arabic so that they can read the Koran. Those who are good in Arabic can go to the universities in the Middle East or Egypt. In addition to their Maldivian name, everybody also has an Arabic name. This is to enable them to make the haj pilgrimage to Mecca. When dealing with foreigners, they use their Arabic name.

Maldivians do not make use of much body language because they are a rather reserved people. Conversations are carried on in a quiet, relaxed tone. An onlooker would have no idea what is going on just from watching two Maldivians talking.

DHIVEHI

Dhivehi is closest to Elu (AY-loo), an ancient form of Sinhalese, the language of Sri Lanka. However, it has also borrowed words from Hindi, Arabic, English, and Bengali. Some language experts believe that the Maldivians first spoke Dhivehi as a form of secret code. As the ancient Maldivians traded mostly with Sri Lankans, they had to modify Sinhalese words or use them with different meanings so that the Sri Lankans would not understand what they were saying among themselves. It was also a way of defining their individuality as a nation so as not to be assimilated and invaded by the Sri Lankans or any other country. In Dhivehi the numbers from 1 to 12 are of Sinhalese origin, while the rest are in Hindi. The names of the days are both Sinhalese and Hindi. Dhivehi has contributed one word to the English language—*atoll*, from *atolhu*. The Maldivians are extremely proud of this.

Dhivehi is the language of the Maldivian administration. In the remote islands it is the only language spoken by the inhabitants. Dhivehi has a number of dialects, particularly in the south, where the dialect has more similarities with Sinhalese. People in Male, for example, do not understand the dialect of Addu Atoll. Until the 1960s Dhivehi was the only medium of instruction in all schools. But today, with the growing need for further education, English is also taught.

Many young people are bilingual in English and Dhivehi.

A CLASS-CONSCIOUS LANGUAGE

Dhivehi is a class-conscious language. There are three classes. The highest level, called "nice language," is used to address members of the upper class and on national radio and television. The second level, which is less formal, is adopted to show respect for elders or to talk to government officials and strangers. Most Maldivians use informal Dhivehi, the third level, in everyday life.

MODERNIZING A LANGUAGE

For official correspondence with other countries and for the benefit of foreigners, the government introduced a Romanized transliteration of Maldivian names and words in 1977 in which the sounds are reproduced using the Roman alphabet. Words are spelled phonetically to produce something that looks familiar to the English speaker. Many words, however, are mere approximations, and there is no correct or even consistent way of spelling local words in English language publications. For example, the word *Dhivehi* itself is sometimes spelled Divehi.

THE WRITTEN LANGUAGE

Dhivehi is written with a script called Thaana (TAR-nah). This script was invented by the national hero Mohammed Thakurufaanu in the 16th century after he threw the Portuguese out of the country. Thaana consists of 24 letters, of which the first nine are forms of Arabic numerals. Vowels are written above the letters in the form of dashes. Thaana is written from right to left, which is similar to Arabic script. Hence a Maldivian book actually starts on what we would consider the last page.

The earliest Dhivehi script was called Evayla (AY-vay-lah). It was written from left to right and contains many characters that are similar to Sinhalese. Evayla also included Arabic words. Another script, called Dhives (DEE-vess), replaced Evayla in the 12th century. Dhives was also written from left to right. Thaana, which replaced Dhives, is written from right to left in order to accommodate the large number of Arabic words imported into Dhivehi. Similar in appearance to shorthand, Thaana looks like a series of tiger paw prints. It resembles Arabic but is fatter, with more squiggles. The oldest example of written Dhivehi is found on a series of ancient copper books called Loamaafaanu (LOW-mar-far-noo). The earliest book dates from 1195.

ENGLISH

Now the second language of most educated Maldivians, English was banned when the country gained independence. Although English has always been taught in Male, it was only taught in private schools, which very few Maldivians could afford. In the 1960s the government added English to the curriculum, making it compulsory for high school students to have a good knowledge of the language in order to pass their examinations.

Today many English words have been adopted into Dhivehi, in particular adjectives or attitudes that did not exist in traditional society. To turn an English word into Dhivehi, Maldivians attach the letter "u" at the end of the word—for instance, *dhoru* (door), *teacharu* (teacher), and *computaru* (computer).

A girl reading a book in the cramped corridor of her home.

DHIVEHI PRONUNCIATION

In Dhivehi, stress always falls on the first syllable of the word. The language does not make use of difficult sounds; any English speaker can learn Dhivehi without having to learn new sounds. Consonants have the same sound as in English. Vowels are pronounced as follows:

a, as in "but"

aa, as in "rather"

ai, as in "cry"

e, as in "bed"

ee, as in "bee"

i, as in "grit"

o, as in "lot"

oa, as in "grow"

u, as in "put"

GREETINGS

Maldivians may not appear to be very courteous to the casual observer because there are not many greeting words in Dhivehi. When meeting an acquaintance, the Maldivian either smiles or nods the head. Some men may shake hands only with other men, but never with a woman. Physical closeness with a person of the opposite sex other than the spouse is not allowed in Islam. Unlike most languages, where strangers or people who are respected are greeted with the titles "Mr.," "Mrs.," or "Ms.," the Maldivian language does not have such forms of address. Even when addressing a relative stranger, Maldivians will not use an honorific.

With the arrival of more foreigners in Maldives, Maldivian sophisticates now use the English word *hello* to greet one another. It is less formal than the Arabic greeting *assalaamu alaikum* (ASS-sahl-lar-moo ah-LAEE-koom). Others use *kihineh* (KEE-he-neh), meaning "How?". Farewells are equally short. *Dhanee* (DAH-nee), which means "going," takes the place of "good-bye." One recent introduction is *shukriyya* (SHOE-kree-yah) for "thank you." Maldivians do not think that it is necessary to thank someone for a favor; they think the person who is doing the favor is only doing his or her duty.

A family in their home. Men and women do not have physical contact with anyone other than their spouses.

NEWSPAPERS

Four daily newspapers are published in Maldives. Tabloid in format, they are between 14 and 16 pages long, with a few pages in English containing a useful digest of the day's main news from international agencies. *Haveeru*, the evening daily, enjoys the widest circulation. Mainly in Dhivehi, it has one

Newspapers are the main source of foreign news for most Maldivians.

or two pages in English. *Haveeru* does not appear on Fridays. The morning paper is called *Aafathis*, meaning "new morning." On Tuesdays it brings out a special English edition. Otherwise only two pages are in English daily, including advertisements for movies. *Miadhu*, which means "today," comes out at noon every day. The newest entrant is *Jazeera*, a daily specializing in finance and sports news. The Maldivian government publishes a weekly newspaper in Dhivehi called *Furadhaana*. Young people read a quarterly magazine, *Dhanfulhi*, with features in both Dhivehi and English. The oldest English language publication is *Maldives News Bulletin*, a weekly issue published by the Maldives News Bureau of the Ministry of Tourism, Arts, and Culture. Since 2008 it can only be viewed online. The majority of Maldivian newspapers also bring out an online edition in both Dhivehi and English. *Minivan News* is an English-language Web-based paper with sharp and incisive reports on the local situation.

RADIO AND TELEVISION

The government-operated Radio Voice of Maldives broadcasts in Dhivehi and English throughout the archipelago around the clock. The English section comes on air between 12:00 P.M. and 2:00 P.M. A number of private radios also operate in Maldives, with Capital Radio 95.6 carrying some BBC World Service programs and DhiFM 95.2 relaying Radio Australia in English. Television Maldives (TVM), which started in 1978, operates two channels that transmit 18 hours of news, current affairs, and variety programs, and 10 hours of entertainment shows respectively. Much of the programming is religious in nature, and the stations take regular breaks for prayer. TVM features Al Jazeera rebroadcasts in English and a daily news segment in English at 9:00 P.M. Two private stations broadcast only in Male.

The Nasheed government has pledged to bring in a new era of media freedom in the country and will relinquish control of television and radio services as well as newspapers. A privatization process is under way to bring about a deregulated media sector that will ensure press freedom and competition.

Satellite dishes in a village.

ARTS

A Maldivian woman embroidering the intricate collar of the Maldivian national dress.

A LTHOUGH MALDIVIAN ARTS ARE not as spectacular as the arts in India or Sri Lanka, local artists have found a variety of ways with their limited raw materials to express themselves.

Because Maldives is a Muslim country and reproduction of the human form is prohibited by Islam, there is no tradition of painting and sculpture. As many Maldivians do have a talent for design, however, many young people are producing contemporary graphic designs.

In the past some islands were famous for stone carving and the artists' talent can still be seen on old gravestones. The carving of

Maldivian handicrafts are very fine in quality and creative in design. Skills are passed down from one generation to another, and Maldivian craftsmen take great pride in their work. The tourist industry has created a great demand for traditional arts and crafts.

Detail of a finely carved gravestone.

calligraphy is also dying out. Old mosques display intricate calligraphy of the scriptures in both stone and wood. Today the Maldivian artistic feelings are seen more widely in arts and crafts. Local handicrafts, which once served a utilitarian purpose, are now produced for the tourist market.

LITERATURE

Maldives does not have much of a literary tradition. Its most prolific writers are Hassan Ahmed Maniku and Maumoon Abdul Gayoom. They have concentrated on the social, religious, economic, and historical aspects of the country. Husain Salahuddin (1881—1948), an attorney general and later chief justice of Maldives, was an influential writer and poet. Maldives does have a rich oral tradition of myths and folk legends, but it is only recently that local folk tales have been published in Dhivehi and English. Most of them are stories of witchcraft and sorcery, while others preach against various sins and transgressions. It will take a few more decades for creative writing to find its place in Maldivian society.

Souvenir T-shirts for tourists are a creative outlet for young painters.

LACQUERWARE

One of the most beautiful products made by Maldivian artisans is lacquerware, wooden objects covered with colored resin. Traditionally lacquered containers were presented as gifts to the sultan. These were mainly bowls, trays, and boxes of various sizes. Modern artisans have

A craftsman working on lacquerware.

added vases, cups, and chess sets to their range. Nevertheless the designs still follow traditional colors and styles.

Many types of wood are used to produce lacquerware, although the traditional pieces are made from the local Alexandrian laurel. The whole process is done by hand, according to age-old practices. First the carver places a block of wood on a wheel that is turned by an assistant pulling a rope forward and backward around a spindle in a steady rhythm. As the wheel turns, the carver quickly chips at the wood with old style tools to give it the desired shape. Next he uses sandpaper to smooth the object, and then pours lacquer on it, while the wheel is turned rapidly. Several colors of lacquer are applied in different layers, and the craftsman will be waiting for each layer to harden before pouring on another color. Common colors are red, yellow, and green on a black background. Once all the layers have set, the carver uses a very sharp tool to make incisions into the various layers so as to produce a pattern. As he cuts away the lacquer, the various colors appear as a motif. Most lacquered objects have abstract floral motifs with a close resemblance to Chinese artwork.

LACQUERWARE FROM THULHAADHOO

The best lacquerware comes from Thulhaadhoo in Baa Atoll. Sitting informally in the shade of the island trees, a few elderly craftsmen keep a skill that has been passed down for generations alive. In the village square, the posts holding up the platform where people meet are intricately covered in lacquer. Islanders love their lacquered plates and use them at religious and family festivals. The most impressive are large, round food boxes used to hold the family dinner on feast days. They have elaborately designed lids.

MALDIVIAN FURNITURE

Maldivians have invented two pieces of furniture that enable them to keep cool and relax. The *undhoali* (OON-dow-lih) and *joli* (JO-lih) are both used outdoors for sitting or reclining. When indoors Maldivians sit and sleep on woven mats.

Undhoali is a type of swing that hangs on the verandah or from a tree in the garden. Made of a wooden platform hanging from an A-frame, it can seat several people. Sometimes called a bed-boat, the *undhoali* can be very elaborate, with a cot-like frieze at its ends and supports at the four corners. It is the perfect piece of furniture for taking a rest in the shade. A combination of sofa, hammock, and fan, the *undhoali* swings gently to lull its occupant to sleep, as the movement produces a slight breeze. Some villagers claim that the movement of the *undhoali* reminds them of the gentle lapping waves.

The *joli* has one of the same aims as the *undhoali*, to cool the occupant. It is a seat made of a rectangular frame with the sitting areas made of nets.

A family sitting on *jolis* outside their house built out of corals.

It feels like sitting in a string shopping bag. The *joli* is divided into three or four sections to form individual, bucket-type seats. It is usually found outside the house, and strangers are welcome to sit down and take a rest while walking from one end of the island to the other.

ARCHITECTURE

Island houses are built of coral, a plentiful raw material in Maldives. Instead of using bricks, Maldivian builders use coral stones cemented to each other with lime. This lime is actually melted coral that is burned slowly in deep pits. Roofs are made of woven coconut leaves. Today more owners choose corrugated iron sheets to cover their houses. Although iron roofs are hotter, they last longer than thatch. Village houses are not painted. They start out white because of the coral and take on a grayish tinge as time passes.

Houses are small with a few rooms, mainly meant for sleeping. Cooking is done in an outbuilding. The veranda and garden serve as the living areas. At the back is a well with a private courtyard. The walls surrounding this courtyard are high because the area around the well serves as an open-air bathroom. At road junctions, the walls have rounded corners. This is a traditional feature that makes it easier for traffic to turn corners.

The most striking example of Maldivian architecture is the Old Friday Mosque in Male. It was built in 1656 with coral stones that were fitted along grooves, not cemented with masonry. The interior is decorated with wood and coral carvings of local flora, and the roof contains 12 domes covered with bright designs in lacquer.

JEWELRY

On special occasions, Maldivian women wear intricately carved heavy silver bracelets and armlets, long thin belts that wrap several times around the waist, silver charm pendants, and gold necklaces. These have remained in the family for generations and point to the genius of the ancient jewelers. Although modern silversmiths and goldsmiths still produce outstanding jewelry, they cannot match their forefathers in brilliance. Most jewelers live in Dhaal Atoll, with goldsmiths on Ribudhoo and silversmiths on Hulhudheli. According to local belief, the sultan banished his chief jeweler to Ribudhoo after the latter was caught substituting gold-plated silver for the sultan's pure gold. The exiled artisan taught his skills to the islanders.

Coral and tortoiseshell jewelry is produced for the tourist market. Skilled craftsmen make beautiful necklaces and bracelets with fish bones decorated with black coral and mother of pearl. Although black coral is endangered and banned from export, it is still fished in Lhaviyani Atoll. Local divers go to a depth of 98 feet (30 m) to harvest the beautiful brittle branches. When cut and polished, they are set into rings, earrings, pendants, and bangles.

Weavers using a narrow loom to weave patterns into cloth.

WEAVING

The most common woven item is *cadjan* (KAH-jan), a mat made from coconut leaves sewn together with rope. It serves as roofing and as fencing. Cadjan mats are also used for sleeping and for lining seats. The finest mat in Maldives is the *kuna* (KOO-nah). It can be as small as a placemat or as large as a mattress. It is a specialty of the women of Huvadhoo Atoll who only use the reeds from their own islands. Collecting the reeds, drying them, and weaving a mat can take weeks. It is mostly a labor of love because the mats do not fetch a very high price in the shops. The reeds are dried in the sun and stained with natural dyes. Colors are muted, ranging from fawn to black. When the reeds are ready, they are woven into intricate abstract designs on a wooden loom. Some women weave on a rope frame pegged out to hold the warp.

Few people still weave textiles, but Eydhafushi in Baa Atoll was once famous for its *feyli* (FAY-lih), a heavy white cotton sarong with brown and black strands. Many old women still wear the *feyli* as an underskirt.

LEISURE

Maldivian boys playing with a toy sailboat. Generally, only young children seek recreation in the sea.

11

LIFE IN THE ISLANDS IS SOMETIMES quite harsh, so for most people, leisure means resting in the shade and enjoying the cool breeze.

While the men gather in the village square for a chat in the late afternoon, the women usually get together during the day when they sweep the streets or clean the beaches. Families swing gently on the *undhaoli* or sit on the *joli* while talking to neighbors or friends.

Many old women like to smoke the *guda-guda* (GOO-dah GOO-dah), a water pipe that makes a gurgling sound, hence the local name. Sitting

The island of Viligili is a short ferry trip from Male. Here Male residents come for weekend picnics, leisurely walks, or a swim in the sea. It is the perfect escape from the overcrowded and stressful capital.

A woman enjoys a smoke on the *guda-guda.*

Scuba diving is an activity that is more popular with tourists than Maldivians.

on a mat, the smoker places the round bottle of water on the ground next to her feet. Two metal tubes are inserted into the lid, one linking the bottle to the tobacco burning in a funnel and the other to a long rubber hose. To smoke she brings the hose to her mouth and inhales the smoke. Many men also like to indulge in conventional cigarette smoking.

SPORTS

Although most foreigners go to Maldives for water sports, especially diving, Maldivians do not look to the sea for recreation. Only young children play in the sea. They do so fully clothed, as dictated by Islamic modesty. Older children do not swim because wearing wet clothes that cling to the body is improper. As is to be expected from a former British protectorate, the two most popular sports in Maldives are soccer and cricket, two typical British games.

CRICKET

Similar to baseball, cricket is played on an oval grass field by two teams of 11 players who take turns to bowl at a wicket defended by a batter from the opposing team. Players are dressed in long-sleeved white shirts and trousers, and batters wear shin pads to protect their legs. Former president Gayoom was a keen cricket player, and his enthusiasm has helped to popularize the game. The season starts in March, and many teams take part in the national tournament.

SOCCER

Soccer is, without doubt, the national sport of Maldives. Every island has a soccer field where young men gather for an informal match in the late afternoon. On Male alone there are more than 30 teams playing in the semi-professional national soccer league. The teams are divided into three

Boys playing soccer. Soccer is one of the most popular games in Maldives.

The Maldivian national team celebrate a goal scored against Sri Lanka during the South Asian Football Federation Cup in 2005.

divisions, and important games are played at the National Stadium. Three main tournaments pit the teams against each other every year. Foreign teams, usually from Sri Lanka, are invited to participate in the President of Maldives Invitation Soccer Cup. Soccer fans who do not live in Male can join in the action "live" through radio and television broadcasts of the main matches. The inter-atoll championship is a big affair, with the entire island, including women and children, turning out for the final. After the game, everybody takes part in a big feast that sprawls out into the streets. A veritable soccer fever grips the entire nation every four years during the soccer World Cup. Soccer is the only sport where Maldives has been able to defeat foreign teams.

Old men playing chess, a game that is highly popular in Maldives.

BOARD GAMES

People in Maldives like to play board games because they are not physically demanding and can be played in the cool shade of a large tree. Chess is a favorite game with older men, who play it fast and with great gusto. However, this is a modified version of the classic game with different rules. Maldivian chess sets, consisting of lacquered chess pieces, are made locally. The chess pieces are yellow and red and are shaped like divots; only the size distinguishes one from the other.

Carrom (KAH-rom), an Arabic game also popular in India and Sri Lanka, is played by younger people, since it involves more dexterity and hand-eye coordination. A form of pool, it uses a large board with pockets in the four corners. Players face one another and shove a flat disk with their forefingers to try and push smaller black or white disks into the pockets. The first one to pocket all his or her disks wins the game. Four persons can play *carrom* in teams of two, with team members facing one another.

Younger children play *ovvalhu* (OH-vah-loo). The board is carved out of a wooden block and has 16 little depressions. Cowry shells are placed in the depressions. It is a good way of teaching children how to count.

LEISURE IN MALE

People in Male have more facilities for leisure. Apart from traditional sports and board games, they can watch television or go to the movies. Two theaters screen movies from India and Hollywood, with all suggestive scenes snipped out by the censors' scissors. Three-hour Hindi epics produced by the studios in Bombay are very popular among Maldivians because they include songs, dances, and drama. American movies are shown in English.

Maldivian girls playing a game of *carrom*.

Bashi (BAH-shi) is an ancient Maldivian game that is popular throughout the islands. Only girls play this sport. In Male young women enjoy a game of bashi *in the parks in the early evening. Played on a kind of tennis court with a net separating the teams, the game consists of bashing a ball over the net while facing away from the opponents. The girls on the opposing team try to catch the ball with their hands. Each team consists of about 11 players. The game derives its name from the handwoven* bashi. *The* bashi *is a kind of bat made from coconut palm leaves and traditionally used to hit the ball. Today, however, most girls use a tennis racket and ball. Although* bashi *is played everywhere, there is no tournament.*

Another ancient game is thin mugoali *(THIN MOO-go-lih), which has been played in the atolls for more than 400 years. This game is very similar to baseball. The objective is to make as many home runs as possible. The base consists of a circle made by rotating on one foot in the sand. The sun-hardened lower part of a coconut leaf stem serves as the bat, and the squarish ball is made of coconut fronds.*

Mandi (MAHN-dee) is a type of primitive lacrosse. The players use long sticks to hurl and catch a small stick without letting it drop on the ground. Young men also like to engage in bai bala *(BY BAH-lah), a Maldivian form of tag wrestling. The player enters a ring and tries to touch the members of the opposite team. If he is not pulled out of the ring by an opponent, the person he has touched is eliminated.*

Many residents of Male like to take a stroll in the cool evening air. Sometimes they hang out at teashops or play *carrom* or chess. Concerts and exhibitions are an occasional treat.

SONG AND DANCE

Despite their Islamic upbringing, Maldivians show little restraint in their songs and dances. It is in their dances that Maldivians express their reserved emotions and acknowledge their varied ancestry. African, Indian, and Arabian influences can be seen in their songs and dances. Traditional songs and dances have not changed over the centuries.

Dances are usually performed to celebrate special occasions and are ritualized around specific ceremonies and rites of passage such as circumcision. Men and women have separate dances that reflect their different activities. Accompaniment is provided mainly by drums, tambourines, bells, and scrapers. Drums are made from a hollow coconut trunk covered with the skin of a ray or with the stomach lining of a shark. Musicians are usually men, especially drummers, but women have also taken to beating pot drums in recent years. The songs that accompany the dance sometimes tell a story if they are in Dhivehi or are just a string of unintelligible sounds, including some African and Arabic words.

FEMALE DANCES

Women mainly take part in three dances: *maafathi neshun* (MAR-fah-tee NAY-shoon), *bandiya jehun* (BAN-dih-yah JAY-hoon), and *bolimalaafath neshun* (BOH-lih-mah-lar-fat NAY-shoon). *Maafathi neshun* is a festival dance performed in national dress. Two rows of 10 women carry bows

Maldivian girls engaged in a traditional dance.

with artificial flowers attached to them. They are accompanied by three drummers and singers, who sing songs that express national feelings and are set to Indian music. *Bandiya jehun* is a harvest and fertility dance similar to the Indian pot dance. The dancers set the rhythm by beating on the metal water pots they carry. To make a louder sound, they wear metal rings on their fingers. The dance is performed in both standing and seated positions. The most important of all women's dances, the *bolimalaafath neshun* originates from the tradition of offering gifts to the sultan. The gift is in the form of shells contained in a small box or vase covered with a bright silk cloth. Twenty-four women, dressed in brightly colored local costumes infused with the scent of burning incense, are required for this dance. As they sing and dance, they form groups of two, three, or four, and they walk toward the sultan to offer him the gift.

MALE DANCES

A male dance in which it is the sultan's turn to offer gifts to the people is *gaa odi lava* (GAR OH-dih LAH-vah). Each dancer carries a stick, and the dancers slowly walk in two rows toward a box containing the gift. While still dancing and singing, they form a circle around the box before taking it away. The rhythm increases as the song and dance progress. *Dhandi jehun* (DAN-dih JAY-hoon) is a stick dance that is performed differently from atoll to atoll. Facing a partner, each dancer holds a stick about 3 feet (1 m) long. As he dances the dancer strikes his stick against the one belonging to his partner. The rhythm is provided by the beating sticks, and the men sing along as they dance. A variation of this dance is the *jehun* (JAY-hoon), which is performed seated. As they strike their sticks, the dancers show off their skill by twisting and gyrating their torsos to the music. *Thaara* (TAR-rah) is a semi-religious song performed in Arabic in fulfillment of a vow. The most common dance is *bodu beru* (BOW-doo BAY-roo), thought to have been introduced to Maldives by Africans in the 12th century. Swaying to the rhythm of loud drums and clapping, dancers leap and jerk as if in a trance, striking almost grotesque poses. *Bodu beru* is usually performed after a hard day's work.

The lyrics of the *bodu beru* have no meaning because they consist of a mixture of Dhivehi, African, and other words.

FESTIVALS

Maldivian women perform a folk dance. Dancing is a part of many Maldivian festivities.

CHAPTER

MALDIVIANS CELEBRATE two types of holidays: national days with a historical significance and religious festivals. All celebrations are community affairs as men, women, and children share in the preparation of food, decorations, and entertainment.

Unlike in most Muslim countries, many religious holidays in Maldives are celebrated over several days of feasting, dancing, and merrymaking. Most festivals involve a blend of the modern with the traditional. Folk dances

Maldivians celebrating with colorful flags and drums.

Not withstanding their strict Muslim faith, Maldivians celebrate festivals with gusto. Feast days are marked with parties, music, and dance. A sense of family pervades as men, women, and children all work together in the preparations. All festivals bring out the Maldivian flag, hanging along the main road or displayed from private homes.

accompanied by traditional instruments can be followed by pop songs. Some villages put on a performance of pot dancers or a *raivaru* recital. All celebrations usually end with a *bodu beru*, the energetic Maldivian dance with an irresistible beat.

KUDA ID

The most important festival in Maldives is Kuda Id, which marks the end of Ramadan, the Islamic fasting month. For one whole month, everyone fasts from sunrise to sunset except the very young children or the physically frail. This is a real test of faith because the climate of Maldives makes it very difficult to go without water for a whole day. In addition Muslims are supposed to abstain from sex and other pleasures, such as smoking, during the month.

As the sun sets, a horn shell is sounded to tell people that they can break their fast. Islanders rush to drink coconut milk or tea and eat some snacks while waiting for their dinner of rice and fish curry. Ramadan food is specially prepared to restore the energy lost during the day. Those who are fasting will wake up before dawn of the next day to eat a meal of rice and fish sauce.

During Ramadan everyone, from children to adults, is expected to fast from sunrise to sundown.

THE NEW MOON

On the 30th day of Ramadan, religious scholars go to sea in a boat to witness the birth of the new moon, which signals the end of the fasting month. The next day is Kuda Id. If they do not see the new crescent, the people carry on fasting one more day until it is confirmed that the new moon has risen. A cannon announces the end of Ramadan in Male.

Maldivians celebrate Kuda Id for three days. The first day starts with a prayer, followed by a special lunch to which family and friends are invited. Children ask their elders for forgiveness, and the whole festival is characterized by a sense of family togetherness. Food and money are given to charity, and everyone exchanges greeting cards. In the afternoon they put on their new clothes for the Id parade. The main streets are filled with colorful bands and marchers.

OTHER RELIGIOUS FESTIVALS

Two lunar months and 10 days after Kuda Id, Maldivians celebrate Bodu Id to mark the hajj pilgrimage to the Muslim holy city of Mecca in Saudi Arabia. All

Maldivians celebrating a festival with dance.

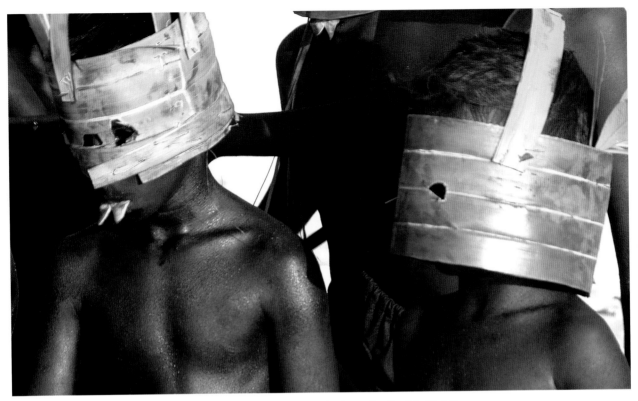

Boys with masks made of leaves during a festival in Maldives.

Muslims try to go on the hajj once in their lifetime for an uplifting spiritual experience. Bodu Id is four days of solid feasting and celebration. People say special prayers and play Bodu Id games. On some islands residents splash each other with water. Many also visit other islands to enjoy the festivities.

The Prophet Muhammad's birthday is another Muslim holiday that is celebrated with great gusto. For three whole days families invite one another to share their food in villages throughout the islands.

PATRIOTISM

Maldivians have a strong sense of national pride; they commemorate all occasions in their history when the nation has triumphed over attempts to curb their sovereignty. All national holidays are celebrated with parades, and various organizations participate in the marching bands. Elaborate fireworks decorate the night sky as the older generation recounts the struggle for independence. In the villages children have their own parade. Smartly dressed they march through the main street watched by their proud parents, neighbors, and other spectators. Houses are decorated with the national flag, and some patriotic young men even paint themselves green and red.

NATIONAL HOLIDAYS

National Day is celebrated on the first day of the third lunar month. It commemorates the end of the Portuguese occupation in 1578. Also associated with the Portuguese occupation is Martyr's Day, which marks the death of Sultan Ali VI at the hands of the Portuguese invaders in 1558. Huravee Day celebrates the overthrow of the Malabars of India who occupied Maldives for a few months in 1752. Independence Day, which marks the end of the British protectorate in 1965, is celebrated on July 26 every year. Republic Day commemorates the founding of the second republic in 1968 and is celebrated in Male with brass band performances and parades. Victory Day falls on November 3. Maldivians celebrate their victory over the Tamil mercenaries from Sri Lanka, who tried to overthrow the government in 1988.

In keeping with the Maldivian zest for festivals, most national holidays last at least two days. The actual day is devoted to official parades, while the next day is for the people to enjoy themselves.

THE RITE OF CIRCUMCISION

The most important rite of passage for boys is circumcision. Mandated by Islam, it is performed when a boy turns six and involves snipping off the foreskin of the sexual organ. Circumcision usually takes place during the December school vacations, and several families get together to defray the cost. While the boys are being circumcised, their relatives massage their feet, and they sing and dance to take the boys' minds off the pain. The boys take about three days to recover. Throughout the three days, sometimes for

A birthday party in the Maldives is a rarity.

a week, the families organize a big party with plenty of entertainment and food. The house is decorated with colorful bright lights, and guests will bring beautiful presents for the boys.

BIRTH AND DEATH

On the islands, it is the medicine man who is in charge of circumcision; children in Male are taken to a doctor.

A newborn baby receives its name on the seventh day after his or her birth. During the ceremony a special prayer is said, and food is given to the poor. On many islands the parents also shave the baby's head for this occasion. Birthdays are not usually celebrated nor even remembered. When a person dies, the burial takes place within 24 hours. The family offers a special prayer followed by a feast on the 40th day after the death.

CALENDAR OF FESTIVALS

Holidays that have a fixed date every year are:

New Year's Day: January 1

Independence Day: July 26

Victory Day: November 3

Republic Day: November 11

Fishermen's Day: December 10

Holidays that follow the Islamic lunar calendar are:

Islamic New Year

National Day

The Prophet Muhammad's Birthday

Huravee Day

Martyr's Day

Kuda Id

Bodu Id

FOOD

A man bringing fresh produce to the main jetty of Male for sale.

A S IN OTHER ASPECTS of life, Maldivian cuisine is the result of various foreign influences. Most dishes tend to be spicy, with curry being a firm favorite. A feature of the Maldivian diet is the lack of green vegetables and fresh fruits. The vegetables and fruit available in the markets are expensive because most of them are imported.

The Maldivian family eats three full meals a day: breakfast, lunch, and dinner. In between they snack on a variety of sweets and other treats.

Men loading bananas onto a boat. Most fresh fruit and vegetables are imported into Maldives.

Rice as well as fish is the staple of Maldivian meals. The latter can be eaten freshly caught, salted, or smoked. Maldive fish is a favorite flavoring ingredient in Maldivian and Sri Lankan cooking. To make Maldive fish, the fish is gutted, boiled, smoked, and sun-dried until it takes on a wood-like appearance. It can keep for ages without refrigeration.

Maldivians eat with their right hand, rolling the food into a ball and pushing it into the mouth with the thumb. Some Male residents use a spoon.

Maldivians enjoy chewing on betel leaves after a meal. This custom, which is a few centuries old, is supposed to aid digestion and freshen the breath. It also acts as a mild stimulant. Maldivians start the habit when they are young. From the age of 14, men and women chew little packets of betel leaves wrapped around areca nut and lime during the day. For this reason Maldivians usually have their teeth stained dark by the red betel juice.

FISH AND COCONUT

Two ingredients predominate in the Maldivian diet: fish and coconut. These two products are plentiful in the country. Fish, usually tuna, is eaten in all its forms: fresh, dried, salted, smoked, or canned. Maldivians even have a fish paste that they spread on bread or mix with rice. They also use the fish paste as a dip for cut fruit. All meals, including breakfast, will include the main staples of fish, rice, and coconut.

A vendor preparing to sell betel in an indoor market.

Apart from fish, Maldivians eat very little meat. Chicken is a real treat and is reserved for special occasions, such as Kuda Id or a circumcision feast. It is usually cooked in curry. Another special treat is *biryani* (BEER-yah-nih), rice cooked with fragrant spices, meat, and potatoes.

CARBOHYDRATES

The main source of carbohydrate for Maldivians is rice. Usually steamed, it is sometimes cooked with coconut milk and chili. As importing rice drains

A Maldivian lunch.

precious foreign exchange, the government is encouraging the population to turn to other starchy foods, especially breadfruit, which grows well in the islands. It is usually cut into thin slices and fried for a snack. Breadfruit curry, called *babukeylu hithi* (BAH-boo-kay-loo HEE-tih), is very popular on some islands. Other locally grown starchy vegetables include taro and sweet potatoes. *Roshi* (ROE-shi) is a type of bread made from flour, water, oil, and salt, and is usually eaten for breakfast.

THE NATIONAL DISH

The national dish is *garudhiya* (GAH-roo-dya), a pungent treacle-like soup with chunks of fresh tuna in it. Maldivians smother their rice with it and accompany the meal with lime juice, chili, and onions. Fish is also fried and cooked in curries. For dry fish curry, small pieces of fresh fish are fried in many spices. Smoked fish is usually eaten for breakfast. It is mixed with coconut, onions, chili, and lime juice, and it is eaten with *roshi*.

Ironically, for a country surrounded by water, Maldives has severe water problems. As the islands are flat, the country has no natural reservoirs at ground level. Rainwater collects at around 6 feet (2 m) underground, and Maldivians draw their fresh water from wells. Sometimes they have to line up for a long time with their pails, awaiting their turn. However, if more water is drawn than supplied by rains, sea water infiltrates the ground and mixes with the fresh water. The water table in Male was dangerously low when the government decided to build desalination plants.

Today Male residents get fresh water piped to their homes. A number of desalination plants built with the help of foreign aid produce enough water for the needs of the island. Resort islands also have their own small desalination plants. Through the process of reverse osmosis, sea water is distilled into pure drinking water. These plants consist of racks of metal cylinders, each containing an inner cylinder made of a polymer membrane. Sea water is pumped into the inner cylinder at high pressure, and the membrane allows the pure water to flow to the outer cylinder from where it is piped away. The Coca-Cola plant in North Male is the only one in the world to use sea water to manufacture its drink—after it has been desalinated, of course.

The other islands have devised their own ways to collect rainwater. Large reservoirs are built on the roofs of schools and mosques, and the islanders collect their fresh water from a tap. In the wake of the 2004 tsunami, many islands received their own desalination plants from international nongovernmental organizations. New lightweight and small-sized plants are so portable that they can be fitted to a boat and provide fresh water to islanders in an emergency.

FOOD PREPARATION

Maldivian women do their cooking in a separate building away from the main house. This is to prevent smoke from getting into the living and sleeping quarters. Although some houses in Male have gas or even electric stoves, most households still use wood-burning stoves. Stoves are placed on the ground, and Maldivian women squat down to do their cooking.

The coconut grater is an important utensil, as all the coconut used in cooking is always freshly grated. The grater is actually a low stool with a sharp jagged blade fixed at one end. The coconut is split in two, and the meat is grated on the jagged blade. The grated coconut collects on a tray placed underneath the blade. When a woman does the grating, she sits side saddle on the stool. If it is a man, he straddles the stool.

While women and children in the islands spend a lot of time collecting firewood for cooking, Male residents buy theirs from the firewood market.

Maldivian women spend a lot of time preparing food. Rice has to be husked in large trays, and stones and seeds have to be discarded. To make coconut honey, they have to grate the coconuts, collect the coconut milk, and stir the pot over the fire for several hours.

MARKETS

Villages do not have markets. In Male, however, the markets along the waterfront are a hive of activity. The most interesting is the fish market. In the late afternoon, when the fishing dhoni return, men rush to unload the fat tuna, bonito, and swordfish and carry them across the road into an open-sided area with a tiled floor. The fish are immediately gutted and cleaned. They are sold on the spot and are taken home in carts or hanging from a bicycle's handlebars. The fish market is kept spotless by daily washing and disinfecting.

Boats docked outside the fish market.

Next to the fish market stands the produce market. Located in a covered building, it sells a limited range of fruits and vegetables, rice, coconuts, eggs, and toddy. The atmosphere is peaceful inside the market as vendors wait quietly for customers to approach them. In the open space in front of the produce market, firewood is sold, including coconut and screwpine wood that are brought in by dhoni from neighboring islands. The vendors are joined by others selling watches, ladles, and underwear.

SHORT EATS

Maldivians are very fond of eating snacks that they call "short eats." (A meal with rice and curry is called a "long eat.") These are like finger foods or cakes. Short eats can be either sweet or savory. Sweets are made from flour, sugar, coconut, and eggs. Savories are based on a mixture of dried smoked fish, grated coconut, lime juice, onion, and chili. Savories are usually small and brown while sweets are light or brightly colored. Short eats are washed down with tea.

A man selling sunglasses and watches at the market in Male.

Gula (GOO-lah) is a favorite short eat. Smoked fish mixed with coconut, onion, ginger, and chili is rolled into a ball and wrapped in pastry, and then fried. Kuli bokibaa (KOO-lih BOH-kih-bar) is made from soaked rice, smoked fish, onion, ginger, chili, and coconut. The mixture is kneaded, baked in a tin, and cut into squares before serving. The Maldivian version of the samosa is called bajiyaa (BAH-jia). This fried pastry triangle is stuffed with canned tuna, onion, chili, and lemon grass.

Foni bokibaa (FOH-nee BOH-kih-bah) is a dessert made from rice flour, coconut, water, sugar, and rose water. It is baked and cut into squares. Huni *foli* (HOO-nee FOH-lih) is *roshi* stuffed with a paste of coconut, honey, and water. It is rolled up like a burrito and fried.

EATING OUT

Most Maldivians do not entertain at home. They prefer to take their guests to a restaurant for a meal. When dining out, the host always pays. It is very bad manners for a guest to reach for the bill and offer to pay. When they have no guests to entertain, few families eat out.

The tea shop is the most common place to eat in Maldives. Frequented by men only, it is a type of cafe that serves short eats and tea. It does not have a menu because all the food is either already set out on the tables or brought by the waiter without the diner having to ask for it. The customer helps himself to whatever he wants and pays for only what he has eaten. As the tables are shared by several persons, it is not easy for the waiter to keep track of what one person has consumed. Tea shops open at 5:00 A.M. and close in the evening. The popular ones don't shut their doors until 1:00 A.M. However, none of them is open for 24 hours. The tea shop

The village tea shop is the place villagers go for tea and simple snacks.

A restaurant with a quirky design.

offers the best opportunity for Maldivian men from all walks of life to socialize and meet friends.

DRINKS

Most islanders drink plain water of course. To wash down their short eats, they drink sweetened hot tea. In Male, Maldivians can choose from a range of soft drinks manufactured locally. Coca-Cola and bitter lemon are very popular. *Suji* (SOO-jih), a local drink made with semolina, coconut milk, nuts, raisins, and a dash of spices, is a refreshing drink. A favorite local drink is toddy. This is the nectar tapped from the crown of the coconut palm at the point where the coconuts grow. Toddy is sweet and natural and tastes better than it smells. The cloudy liquid can be drunk immediately after it has been tapped, and that is how Maldivians like it. If it is left for a while, the sugar starts to ferment, and it becomes slightly alcoholic. Every island has a toddy tapper. However, toddy is becoming scarcer now because young people do not want to become toddy tappers. They see it as a socially humble job.

BARABO PIRINEE (PUMPKIN PUDDING)

5 cups (1¼ kg) pumpkin, grated

1 cup (250 g) yellow raisins

½ cup (125 g) flour

1 cup (250 g) chopped nuts

1 cup (250 ml) water

1 can condensed milk

Vanilla flavoring to taste

Boil water in a pan. Add pumpkin and cook until soft. Stir in raisins and cook on low heat for a couple of minutes. Add milk, vanilla flavoring, and nuts, and stir well. Mix flour with a little water and add to the pumpkin mixture. Cook until thick and consistent. Serve the pudding warm or chilled.

ROSHI (MALDIVIAN ROTI)

1½ cups (192 g) plain flour
3 tablespoons (45 ml) vegetable oil
salt
½ cup (125 ml) boiling hot water

Sift flour in large mixing bowl and add a generous pinch of salt. Make a well in the center and add the oil. Slowly add the hot water and stir with a spoon. Once it becomes clumpy, let the mixture cool. When still slightly warm, knead the dough until smooth and soft. Divide the dough into six to eight balls. Roll each dough ball until it is flat and as thin as possible. Heat a large frying pan, and put the roshi in once it is hot. Flip the roshi over once it begins to puff a little. Serve with curry.

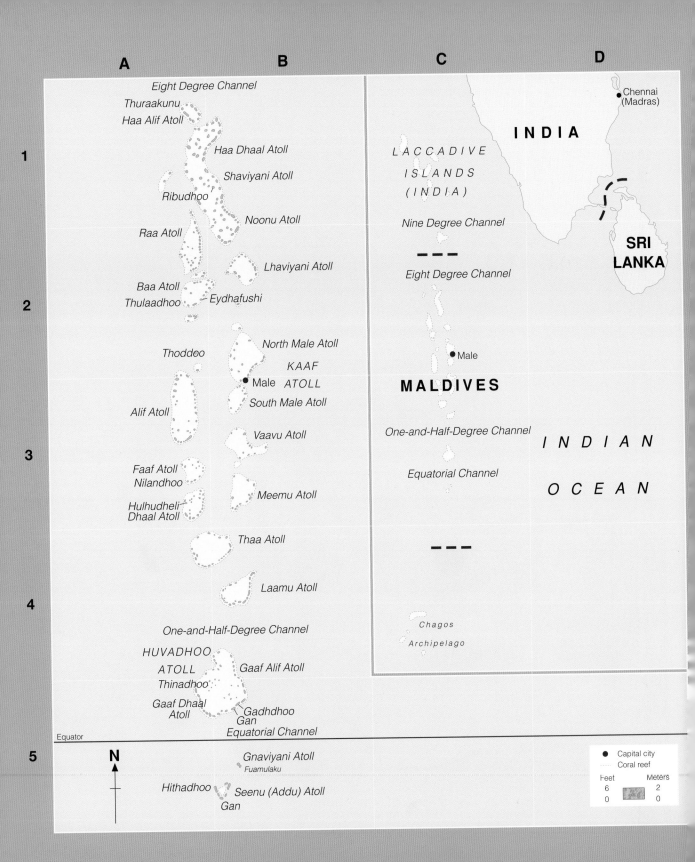

A **B** **C** **D**

1

2

3

4

5

Eight Degree Channel
Thuraakunu
Haa Alif Atoll
Haa Dhaal Atoll
Shaviyani Atoll
Ribudhoo
Noonu Atoll
Raa Atoll
Lhaviyani Atoll
Baa Atoll
Thulaadhoo — Eydhafushi

North Male Atoll
Thoddoo
KAAF
Male   ATOLL
South Male Atoll
Alif Atoll
Vaavu Atoll
Faaf Atoll
Nilandhoo
Meemu Atoll
Hulhudheli
Dhaal Atoll
Thaa Atoll
Laamu Atoll

One-and-Half-Degree Channel
HUVADHOO
ATOLL   Gaaf Alif Atoll
Thinadhoo
Gaaf Dhaal
Atoll   Gadhdhoo
Gan
Equatorial Channel

Equator

Gnaviyani Atoll
Fuamulaku
Hithadhoo   Seenu (Addu) Atoll
Gan

LACCADIVE
ISLANDS
(INDIA)

Nine Degree Channel

– – –

Eight Degree Channel

Male

MALDIVES

One-and-Half-Degree Channel

Equatorial Channel

– – –

Chagos
Archipelago

Chennai
(Madras)

INDIA

SRI
LANKA

INDIAN

OCEAN

N

Capital city
Coral reef

Feet   Meters
6   2
0   0

MAP OF MALDIVES

Alif Atoll, A3

Baa Atoll, A2

Chagos
 Archipelago, C4
Chennai (Madras),
 D1

Eight Degree
 Channel, A1, B1
Eight Degree
 Channel, C2
Equator, A5, B5,
 C5, D5
Equatorial Channel,
 B5
Equatorial Channel,
 C3
Eydhafushi, A2

Faaf Atoll, A3
Fuamulaku, B5

Gaaf Alif Aoll, B4
Gaaf Dhal Atoll, A5
Gadhdhoo, B4
Gan (Seenu Atoll), B5
Gan, B5
Gnaviyani Atoll, B5

Haa Alif Atoll, A1
Haa Dhaal Atoll, B1
Hithadhoo, B5
Hu Vadhoo Atoll,
 A4—A5, B4—B5

Hulhudheli Dhaal
 Atoll, A3

India, C1, D1—D2
Indian Ocean, D3

Laccadive Islands
 (India), C1
Lhaviyani Atoll, B2

Maldives, C2—C3
Male, B3
Male, C2
Meemy Atoll, B3
Nilandhoo, A3

Nine Degree
 Channel, C1—C2
Noonu Atoll, B1
North Male Atoll,
 B2

One and Half
 Degree Channel,
 A4, B4
One and Half
 Degree Channel,
 C3

Raa Atoll, A2
Ribudhoo, A1, B1

Seenu (Addu) Atoll,
 B5
Shaviyani Atoll, B1
South Male Atoll, B3

Sri Lanka, D1—D2

Thaa Atoll, B4
Thinadhoo, A5
Thoddoo, A2
Thulaadhoo, A2
Thuraakunu, A1

Vaavu Atoll, B3

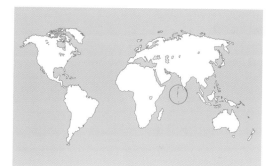

ECONOMIC MALDIVES

Services

✈ Airports

🧍 Tourism

Manufacturing

🏭 Boat building

🍾 Bottling plant

🪸 Coral handicrafts

🧥 Cotton weaving

🐟 Fish processing

💎 Jewelry

☕ Lacquerware

▥ Mat weaving

Agriculture

🫐 Fruits

🥔 Yam

ABOUT THE ECONOMY

OVERVIEW

The Maldivian economy is very dependent on tourism and is thus badly affected by slowdowns in European countries, its main market. After rebounding from the 2004 tsunami, which caused widespread damage to resorts, the country entered a recession in 2008 as part of the global economic crisis. Facing a balance of payments crisis caused by excessive government spending and declining revenues, Maldives is in negotiations with the International Monetary Fund for a $60 million standby loan. Over the years, Maldives has received financial help from multilateral development organizations such as the UN Development Program, the Asian Development Bank, and the World Bank, as well as from individual donor countries such as Japan, India, Australia, and European and Arab countries.

GROSS DOMESTIC PRODUCT (GDP)
$1.674 billion (2009 estimate)

GDP PER CAPITA
$4,200 (2009 estimate)

CURRENCY
Rufiyaa
1 rufiyaa = 100 laari
U.S.$1 = Rf12.8 (February 2010)

GROWTH RATE
-4 percent (2009 estimate)

INFLATION
7.3 percent (2009 estimate)

MAIN EXPORTS
Fish and garments

MAIN IMPORTS
Food, petroleum products, ships, machinery, and consumer goods

LABOR FORCE
144,000 (2009 estimate)

TOURISM
683,012 arrivals (2008)

MAIN TRADE PARTNERS
Singapore, India, Malaysia, Sri Lanka, Thailand, United Arab Emirates, United Kingdom, Italy, and Germany

AGRICULTURAL PRODUCTS
Coconuts, corn, sweet potatoes, and fish

NATURAL RESOURCES
Fish, coconut, and beaches

CULTURAL MALDIVES

Thakurufaanu Memorial
The birthplace of Maldivian hero Mohammed Thakurufaanu was turned into a museum in 1986. The restored wooden palace dates from the 16th century and contains various items of furniture from the different eras. A modern monument, the Bodu Thakurufaanu Memorial Center, serves as a place of study for scholars and contains a library with books on Islam and the history of Maldives.

Grand Friday Mosque
The largest mosque in Maldives was built with help from various Muslim states. Its golden dome dominates the Male skyline and its white marble façade is striking in its plainness. The main prayer hall displays beautiful woodcarvings and Arabic calligraphy done by Maldivian craftsmen.

Old Friday Mosque
The oldest mosque in the country dates from 1656. Built on the foundations of an ancient temple, it faces the setting sun instead of northwest toward Mecca. The interior is famed for its lacquer work and intricate wood carvings. One long panel, dating from the 13th century, commemmorates the introduction of Islam in Maldives.

Aasaari Miskiiy
The second-oldest mosque in Maldives was built in the 12th century, with stones from an ancient temple which was possibly of Hindu origin. The insides of the mosque are heavily decorated with Arabic carvings.

Maa Badhige
This 49-foot- (15-m-) high mound is the remnant of a hawitta, a stone structure dating from Maldives's prehistory.

National Museum
Housed in a new building within the former sultan's palace grounds, the museum displays a collection of artifacts previously owned by the sultans: ornaments and costumes, weapons, lacquer bowls and trays, and a throne. Other interesting exhibits include pre-Islamic stone carvings collected by Thor Heyerdahl.

Hawitta
This giant black dome, believed to be the remnant of a Buddhist stupa, used to be a landmark for boats navigating between the atolls.

War memorial
Gan served as a British air base from 1956 to 1976. The memorial lists the Indian army regiments which served here, commemorating those who died in the service of the nation. Two big guns flanking the memorial formed part of the defenses of Addu Atoll in World War II.

Kedeyre Mosque
Built on the beach, this old mosque is a prime example of great workmanship. A beautiful sunken bath is enclosed by well-fitting cut stone that probably allowed the water to filter through. The mosque is surrounded by beautifully carved tombstones.

ABOUT THE CULTURE

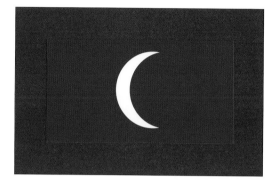

OFFICIAL NAME
Dhivehi Raajjeyge Jumhuriyya, or Republic of Maldives

CAPITAL
Male

TOTAL AREA
34,750 square miles (90,003 square km)

LAND AREA
115 square miles (298 square km)

POPULATION
396,334 (July 2009 estimate)

NUMBER OF ISLANDS
1,190

ADMINISTRATIVE ATOLLS
Alif, Baa, Dhaal, Faaf, Gaaf Alif, Gaaf Dhaal, Gnaviyani, Haa Alif, Haa Dhaal, Kaafu, Laamu, Lhaviyani, Meemu, Noonu, Raa, Seenu, Shaviyani, Thaa, and Vaavu

MAJOR LANGUAGES
Dhivehi and English

ETHNIC GROUPS
Maldivians, Givaaveru, Sri Lankans, and South Indians

RELIGION
Islam

BIRTHRATE
14.55 births per 1,000 population (2009 estimate)

DEATH RATE
3.65 deaths per 1,000 population (2009 estimate)

INFANT MORTALITY RATE
29.53 deaths per 1,000 live births (2009 estimate)

FERTILITY RATE
1.9 children born per woman (2009 estimate)

LIFE EXPECTANCY
Total population: 73.97 years (2009 estimate)
Male: 71.78 years
Female: 76.28 years

TIME LINE

IN MALDIVES	IN THE WORLD
1117 King Sri Mahabarana, first king of Maldives, starts Theemuge Dynasty.	
1153 Islam is adopted as national religion.	**1206–1368** Genghis Khan unifies the Mongols and starts conquest of the world. At its height, the Mongol Empire under Kublai Khan stretches from China to Persia and parts of Europe and Russia.
1558 Portuguese occupation of Maldives	
1573 Mohammed Thakurufaanu drives Portuguese out and becomes first sultan.	
1752 Malabar Indians invade but are expelled after four months. Hassan Manikufaan founds Huraage Dynasty.	**1776** U.S. Declaration of Independence
1887 Maldives becomes a self-governing British protectorate, with the sultans continuing to rule.	**1789–99** The French Revolution
1932 First Maldivian constitution curbs the sultan's powers.	**1914** World War I begins.
	1939 World War II begins.
1953 Declaration of Maldives as a republic. Amin Didi becomes the first president.	**1945** The United States drops atomic bombs on Hiroshima and Nagasaki, Japan. World War II ends.
1954 Amin Didi is overthrown and sultanate restored.	
1957 Ibrahim Nasir is elected prime minister.	
1959 Three southernmost atolls—Addu, Huvadhoo, and Gnaviyani—declare independence as United Suvadive Republic.	
1963 United Suvadive Republic is crushed by Maldivian government.	

IN MALDIVES	IN THE WORLD
1965	
Protectorate is lifted and Maldives gains full independence from Great Britain.	
1968	
Sultanate abolished and Maldives becomes a republic again. Nasir is elected president.	
1978	
Maumoon Abdul Gayoom is elected president.	
1988	
Coup attempt by Sri Lankan mercenaries is quickly foiled with Indian assistance.	**1997**
1998	Hong Kong is returned to China.
El Niño phenomenon causes water temperatures to rise above 89°F (32°C), killing off vital algae and bleaching coral.	
	2001
	Terrorists crash planes into New York, Washington D.C., and Pennsylvania.
	2003
	War in Iraq begins.
2004	**2004**
Indian Ocean tsunami wipes out many towns and villages, leading to abandonment of several islands.	Eleven Asian countries hit by giant tsunami, killing at least 225,000 people.
2005	**2005**
Parliament votes to allow multiparty elections after a campaign for democracy.	Hurricane Katrina devastates the Gulf Coast of the United States.
2007	
Bomb explodes in Sultan's Park in Male, injuring 12 tourists.	
2008	**2008**
First democratic election in Maldives brings Mohammed Nasheed to power, toppling Gayoom.	Earthquake in Sichuan, China, kills 67,000 people.
	2009
	Outbreak of flu virus H1N1 around the world.

GLOSSARY

atolhu varin (AH-toh-loo VAH-rin)
The administrator for an atoll.

bandiya jehun (BAN-dih-yah JAY-hoon)
Pot dance performed by very young women.

bodu beru (BOW-doo BAY-roo)
Energetic dance performed by men on special
occasions or after a hard day's work.

circumcision
Removing the foreskin of the male sexual
organ.

dhevi (DAY-vi)
Spirits that live in objects such as the sky, the
trees, or the sea.

Dhives (DEE-vess)
A written form of the Maldivian language.

dhoni (DOE-nih)
A wooden boat with a distinctive curved prow
used for fishing and transportation.

feyli (FAY-lih)
A heavy white cotton sarong with brown and
black strands.

ghaazee (HAR-zee)
A religious leader.

gula (GOO-lah)
A fish ball wrapped in pastry and fried.

hajj
The pilgrimage to Mecca that should be done
at least once in the lifetime of every Muslim.

hakim
A traditional medicine man or woman.

joli (JO-lih)
A seat made of a wooden frame with a net.

Majlis (MADGE-liss)
Government assembly.

nakaly (NAH-kah-lih)
A calendar based on changes in weather, and
the rising and setting of the stars, the sun,
and the moon.

Ramadan
The Muslim fasting month when no food
or drink may be consumed from sunrise to
sunset.

Redin
A mythical light-skinned people who
worshiped the sun. They are thought to be
the original inhabitants of Maldives.

Thaana (TAR-nah)
The written script of the Maldivian language.

undhoali (OON-dow-lih)
A type of outdoor swing used for sitting and
sleeping.

FOR FURTHER INFORMATION

Books

Coleman, Neville. *Wildlife Guide: Maldives*. Springwood, Queensland, Australia: Neville Coleman's Underwater Geographic, 2006.

Forbes, Andrew and Bishop, Kevin. *Maldives: Kingdom of a Thousand Isles*. Hong Kong: Odyssey Publications, 2004.

Films

Soaring the Maldives Reef. Howard Hall Productions, 2010.

Music

Various artists. *Haven Fushi Maldives*. 2007.

BIBLIOGRAPHY

Books

Masters, Tom. *Maldives*. London: Lonely Planet, 2009.

Websites

CIA World Fact Book. www.cia.gov/library/publications/the-world-factbook/geos/mv.html

Ministry of Housing, Transport and Environment. www.environment.gov.mv

The President's Office. www.presidencymaldives.gov.mv/4/

www.guardian.co.uk/environment/gallery/2009/jan/03/maldives-waste-turns-paradise-into-dump

www.guardian.co.uk/world/audio/2008/nov/10/randeep-ramesh-maldives-climate-change

www.visitmaldives.com/en

INDEX

INDEX